RMS TITANIC

THE WIDER STORY

The Launch of the *Titanic*

Belfast was 'en fete' on the last day of May, when the White Star Line's newest mammoth, the Titanic was launched from the yard of Messrs. Harland & Wolff. As might be expected the ceremony was carried out according to time table without a hitch. So carefully had all the details been thought out and arranged for, that the sound of a whistle and the clanging of a bell, followed by two sharp reports of a rocket were sufficient to signal into motion the hydraulic power that sent this 45,000 ton liner to her home on the ocean wave. Let us hope that the career of the Titanic may prove in every respect as successful and free from trouble as her launch.

From *The Railway & Travel Monthly*, July 1911

Dedicated to:
Chief Officer Henry Tingle Wilde, 1872–1912
First Officer William McMaster Murdoch, 1873–1912
Sixth Officer James Paul Moody, 1887–1912
Purser Hugh Walter McElroy, 1874–1912

RMS TITANIC
THE WIDER STORY

PATRICK MYLON

The
History
Press

First published 2016

The History Press
The Mill, Brimscombe Port
Stroud, Gloucestershire, GL5 2QG
www.thehistorypress.co.uk

British Library Cataloguing in Publication Data.
A catalogue record for this book is available from the British Library.

ISBN 978 0 7509 6136 3

Typesetting and origination by The History Press
Printed in China

CONTENTS

FOREWORD

RMS *Titanic* departed Southampton, at the start of her maiden and only voyage, on Wednesday 10 April 1912. Calling next at Cherbourg and Queenstown (Cobh), she sailed out into the Atlantic towards her destination, New York, carrying over 2,200 passengers and crew. On the night of Sunday 14 April she struck an iceberg at 11.40 p.m. and sank two hours and forty minutes later. Over 700 survivors in lifeboats heard more than 1,500 men, women and children struggling for their lives in the freezing cold water, calling for help that never came. Most of them would be dead within the hour.

Did they know that their vessel had received warning messages of ice ahead? Did they know that the ship was travelling faster that night than at any time in her career, other than on her trials, and that was accepted as 'usual practice'? Did they know that no extra lookout precautions had been taken? Did they know that, because of outdated government regulations, their vessel carried insufficient lifeboats for all those on board? I suspect not.

RMS *Titanic* was the second of three planned liners for the American-owned White Star Line express service between the UK and New York. Her virtually identical (except for an open promenade deck) sister ship, *Olympic*, had sailed on her uneventful maiden voyage in June 1911 and it was she that had attracted the attention of the European and American press – so far. *Titanic* was an attractive ship but so were *Olympic* and her Cunard Line competitors, *Lusitania* and *Mauretania*, all offering equally impressive facilities to their passengers. By 1913 *Olympic* and *Titanic* had lost the title 'Largest Ships in the World' to the first of Germany's giant trio.

THE WIDER STORY

Contemplating this publication, I thought to myself, 'What more can possibly be written about this ship?' Not a lot, actually, but what about her sister ship, the ships stranded in Southampton by a coal strike, the railway stations and the boat trains, the vessels that sent ice warnings and those that responded to the distress calls? I have, of necessity, told the basic story of the ill-fated vessel but have tried to use rarely, if ever, seen illustrations from my collection of postcards, White Star Line memorabilia and paintings.

Many readers will already know the story of RMS *Titanic* backwards, but I hope that you also will enjoy and find interesting the contents of this book. For those wishing to read further, in more detail, I can recommend the publications listed in the Bibliography section, as well as the excellent 'Encyclopedia Titanica' website.

Patrick Mylon
London 2015

ACKNOWLEDGEMENTS

I must thank: Caroline Mylon and Iain Yardley for, once again, much encouragement, technological advice, assistance and patience! Emanuel Silberstein and Patti Aronsson of Washington DC for their friendship and enthusiasm for all things White Star! Amy Rigg, Chrissy McMorris, Glad Stockdale, Darren Lusty and all at The History Press for, once again, their professionalism, advice and design. Neil Egginton and Simon Fisher for kindly allowing me to illustrate using their paintings. Mr Ron Hancock (Port Ambassador, Associated British Ports, Southampton) for his kind and enthusiastic assistance.

All the following assisted greatly with copyright negotiations: Patrick Wingrove, Illustrated London News Ltd; Anne Gleave; Merseyside Maritime Museum; Alyssa Langlais, Peabody Essex Museum; Stephen Atkinson, Rex Features; Karin Tucker, *Scientific American*.

For their long-time friendship, knowledge, enthusiasm and encouragement: Andrew Aldridge, the late Steve Booth, Peter and Jan Boyd-Smith, Neil and Jo Egginton, Richard Faber, Simon and Pauline Fisher, Hank Grossman, Brian Hawley, Mike and Toni Peach, Eric Sauder, Russ and Sandy Upholster.

one

COMPETITION AND CONSTRUCTION

Germany and the United Kingdom dominated the North Atlantic in the early twentieth century, the UK being represented by the Cunard Steamship Company and rival Oceanic Steam Navigation Company (White Star Line).

British businessman Thomas Ismay, recognising the growth of traffic to North America, founded the White Star Line in 1869 and immediately placed an order for four steam-powered vessels, followed by a further two, with Belfast shipbuilders Harland and Wolff. The result of Ismay's intention to offer a reliable service of comfort and speed was to dominate the market between the UK and the USA, two of the richest nations in the world. Then began decades of competition between White Star and Cunard, each company building larger and larger vessels.

76 – Le " Kaiser Wilhelm II ", à son arrivée à Cherbourg

Le plus grand et le plus rapide bateau du monde : longᵣ 215ᵐ, 40.000 chevaux vapeur. — Equipage : 650 hommes. — Passagers : 1.760. — 950 cabines, 810 dans l'entrepont. — Jaugeant 20.000 tonnes. - Vitesse 23 ½ milles par heure.

Collection P. B., Cherbourg

One of Germany's early transatlantic liners, *Kaiser Wilhelm II*, arriving at Cherbourg.

After the initial order of six ships, White Star began to order their vessels in pairs, each to be larger and more comfortable than before. The first pair, *Britannic* and *Germanic*, were followed by *Teutonic* and *Majestic*, all competing with vessels of the Cunard Line for the speed record. In 1893 the record was captured by Cunard's *Campania*, never again to be held by the White Star Line. The names allocated to White Star vessels were suffixed by 'ic' and Cunard chose the suffix 'ia', continuing until the merged Cunard-White Star Line named *Queen Mary* in 1936.

Germany dominated European continental travel to North America with the Hamburg America Line (HAPAG) and North German Lloyd (NDL). Their liners were noted for elegant, some would say elaborate, interiors and also speed. Emigration reached a high in the first decade of the twentieth century with over a million people being carried to the New World in 1907.

The year 1899 brought the death of Thomas Ismay, the maiden voyage of the world's largest liner, *Oceanic*, and White Star's decision to compete no longer for the speed record, but concentrate on reliability, comfort and size. Plans for a sister to *Oceanic* were cancelled and, in 1901, the first of the 'Big Four', *Celtic*, was introduced.

Meanwhile, across the Atlantic, the American financier J. Pierpont Morgan, having created the International Mercantile Marine (IMM) group of shipping companies, and despite already owning some British shipping

North German Lloyd's *Kronprinzessin Cecilie*. Another reason for Britain to compete! (Real Photographs)

White Star's *Celtic*, 21,035grt, first (1901) of the 'Big Four', and water boat *Pontic*.

Cunard Line's *Lusitania* on her trials, 1907. Britain retaliates! (Robertson, Gourock)

lines, had set his sights on Cunard and White Star, hoping to monopolise the growing transatlantic trade. In 1902 the IMM acquired a majority holding in White Star Line, purchasing the allocations of Thomas Ismay's family. Ismay's son, J. Bruce Ismay, initially opposed the sale.

The White Star Line had now become an American-owned company, but US law required that all US-registered vessels be built in the USA; as such, the ships of White Star continued to be registered in Liverpool, UK. Cunard and France's Compagnie Générale Transatlantique resisted acquisition and approached their governments for assistance. Cunard was offered a subsidy for two large express liners with the proviso that, in time of war, they were to be used for the transportation of troops or cargo.

The second of White Star's 'Big Four', *Cedric*, followed in 1903, *Baltic* in 1904 and, finally, *Adriatic* in 1907, each being slightly larger than the last. On the day of *Adriatic*'s launch in Belfast, 20 September 1906, the second of Cunard's subsidised liners, *Mauretania*, was launched at the yards of Swan Hunter on the river Tyne, and her sister *Lusitania* at the yards of John Brown on the Clyde on 7 June.

After the launch of *Adriatic* White Star moved its express transatlantic service from Liverpool to Southampton. With an ever-increasing number of emigrants travelling each year to the USA, it was decided that Southampton offered not only a more convenient departure point from London, but facilitated a call en route at Cherbourg to capture a greater share of the European market.

It is often thought that the concept of super liners, to outclass any competition, was arrived at during a dinner at the London home of W.J. Pirrie (Harland and Wolff) attended by J. Bruce Ismay (White Star Line). However, plans were already afoot prior to this meeting.

White Star had asked Harland and Wolff to look into the design of two large liners and the builders had begun work on the new slipways by the late spring of 1907. Harland and Wolff submitted designs to White Star Line, who approved them in July 1908.

Following White Star's practice of naming its vessels prior to launch, it was announced that the first of the new liners would be named *Olympic* (Yard No. 400), followed by *Titanic* (Yard No. 401). Each vessel would cost £1.5 million and, at 45,000 tons, they were almost half as large again as Cunard's *Lusitania* and *Mauretania*. They were to be nearly 100ft longer, at just over 882ft, have a width of 92½ft, a maximum speed of 24 knots and a service speed of 22 knots. They would be faster than their White Star predecessors, the 'Big Four', but, allowing for the company policy of 'size and comfort over speed', not as fast as their Cunard competitors. The slightly lower speed meant that coal consumption was lower, and *Olympic* and *Titanic* would offer a greater degree of comfort as well as a smoother crossing; nevertheless, the two ships would still be faster than most crossing the Atlantic. The two liners were each to have bunkers with a capacity of 8,000 tons of coal. Passenger capacity was just under 2,500 with 900 crew and each vessel was insured for £1 million ($5 million).

Mauretania, distinguishable by many ventilator cowls, joined her sister *Lusitania* months later, in 1907. (C.R. Hoffmann)

1027. - SAINT-NAZAIRE. - Chantiers et Ateliers de l'Atlantique. - Le Paquebot *France* en achèvement
Long. 218ᵐ, larg. 23ᵐ, jauge 27.000 tonnes, 4 hélices actionnées par des turbines, vitesse 23 nœuds. L'appareil évaporatoire se compose de 4 cheminées, 120 foyers, les cheminées de forme elliptique ont 34ᵐ de hauteur, 5ᵐ30 au grand axe, 4ᵐ10 au petit axe.

Collection Delaveau, St-Nazaire

France's namesake completing at Saint-Nazaire, 1912. (Delaveau)

The construction of a third vessel, enabling White Star to offer a three-ship service providing weekly departures from Southampton and New York, was envisaged.

The word 'unsinkable' was mentioned twice, in advance publications, but each time was accompanied by a qualification. White Star Line, in 1910, stated that 'as far as it is possible to do so, these two vessels are designed to be unsinkable' and the *Shipbuilder* magazine, in 1911, referred to *Olympic* and *Titanic* as being 'practically unsinkable'.

Each ship had three propellers, the outer two being driven by two enormous reciprocating engines with a daily coal consumption of approximately 620 tons. The surplus steam from these two engines powered a low-pressure turbine driving the centre propeller forward of the rudder.

This three-propeller system was decided upon after a trial between the liners *Laurentic* and *Megantic*, built in 1908–09 by Harland and Wolff for White Star's joint Canadian service with the Dominion Line, which was also within the IMM combine. *Laurentic*, powered by three propellers, proved to be more efficient than *Megantic*, which had two outer propellers only. The centre propeller improved the overall efficiency of the vessel but was not reversible, and this may have affected the ship's handling. It is thought that *Olympic* was provided with a centre solid four-bladed propeller, but that of *Titanic* was three-bladed. The outer propellers on each vessel were furnished with three screw-on blades.

White Star's *Laurentic*, 14,892grt, 1908. Her three-propeller system, more efficient than that of her two-propeller sister *Megantic*, was utilised for the Olympic-class liners. She was sunk with serious loss of life as a troopship in January 1917. (Priestley & Co.)

Olympic (centre) and *Titanic* (right) under construction at Belfast. (Doherty)

Queen's Island, Belfast.

Toward the end of 1906 work began at Harland and Wolff to replace three old slipways with two new 1,000ft slips, above which work commenced on the huge Arroll gantry in 1907.

Approximately 15,000 men worked on the construction of the two ships initially three months apart, *Olympic* being the first. The men at Harland and Wolff worked a five-and-half-day week. Saturday afternoons and Sundays were quiet times at the yard compared to the weekly racket of the hydraulic machines. The workforce was supervised by Alexander Carlisle, closely involved in the design of the vessels, assisted by Thomas Andrews (assistant shipyard manager) who took over after Carlisle's retirement on 30 June 1910. Andrews, actively involved in the construction of White Star's 'Big Four' vessels, worked closely with Harland and Wolff's senior naval architect Edward Wilding.

The keel of *Titanic* was laid on Slip No. 3, next to her sister on No. 2, on 31 March 1909.

The two vessels were constructed on the usual 'cost plus' basis established between Harland and Wolff and White Star, requiring Harland and Wolff to build each ship using the best possible materials, adding their commission (usually 4 per cent) to the net price. An additional proviso was that Harland and Wolff would not build for the competition.

Each ship had eight main decks: Lower (G), the lowest in the hull to have portholes; Middle (F); Upper (E); Saloon (D); Shelter (C); Bridge (B); Promenade (A); and, finally, the Boat Deck.

Four large funnels sat atop the boat deck. The forward funnel vented the smoke from boiler rooms 5 and 6; the second funnel, boiler rooms 3 and 4; and the third funnel, boiler rooms 1 and 2. The fourth provided exhaust from the ship's galleys, as well as ventilation to the engine room.

The hull of each ship was divided by fifteen transverse bulkheads, one of which went as high as the floor of C deck, seven to D deck, six to E deck and one to F deck. Many of these bulkheads contained openings and passageways sealed from the bridge by closing watertight doors. Compartment 1 (forward) contained the fore peak tank, 2 and 3 for cargo, 4 for coal and cargo and 5 through 10 contained boiler rooms 6 through 1. Compartment 11 contained the two enormous

White Star Line advertises its new vessels.

Comparison to tall buildings.
(*Scientific American*)

| Bunker Hill Shaft. | Philadelphia City Hall. | Washington Monument. | Metropolitan Tower. | Woolworth Building. | S. S. Olympic, 882½ Feet. | Cologne Cathedral. | The Great Pyramid. | St. Paul's, London. |

COMPARISON OF THE "OLYMPIC," 882½ FEET IN LENGTH, WITH SOME TALL BUILDINGS OF THE WORLD

Launch of *Olympic*, 1910.
(*Scientific American*)

reciprocating engines, 12 the turbine, 13 for electrical machinery, 14 for refrigerated cargo, 15 for general cargo and 16 the stern.

Despite the majority of the bulkheads only reaching as high as D or E decks, the compartment division would have satisfied today's Safety of Life at Sea (SOLAS) requirements. The two vessels could survive with any two adjacent compartments flooded. The bulkhead divisions reached high enough to satisfy Britain's Board of Trade, their surveyors making nearly 3,000 inspection visits during the construction of the two vessels.

The two masts on each ship, forward and main, provided support for rigging and the radio aerial. The crow's nest was attached to the forward mast and fitted with a telephone and an alarm bell overhead.

The British Board of Trade regulations required that sixteen lifeboats be carried on each vessel. The two ships each carried fourteen sixty-five-person capacity lifeboats, two emergency cutters

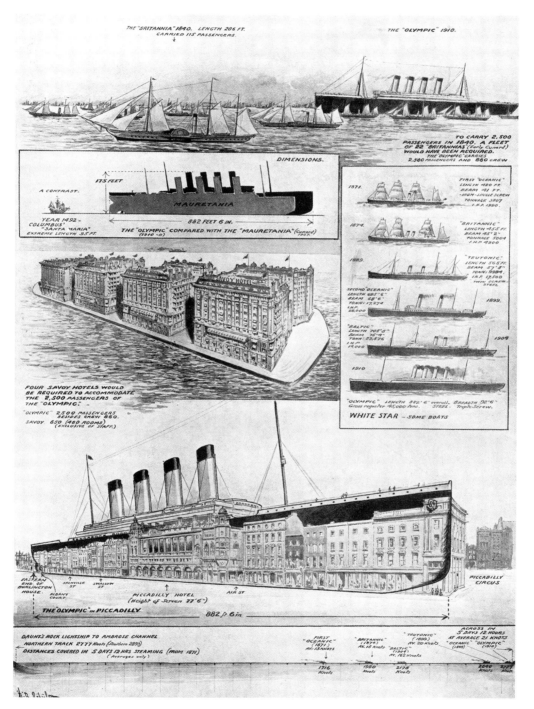

Britain learns of White Star's new vessels. (London Illustrated News Ltd)

DUKE OF ALBANY, FLEETWOOD.

each with a capacity of forty and four collapsible lifeboats each capable of holding up to forty-seven persons. The 'collapsible' boats would be fitted into the Welin davits, after the main lifeboat had departed. Each set of davits could handle up to three boats, instead of the initial one, as the designer at the time, Alexander Carlisle, had anticipated that eventually the Board of Trade would increase the lifeboat requirement considerably and thus the davits were installed accordingly. Each vessel was also supplied with over 3,500 life jackets, 36 socket distress signals (rockets) and 48 life rings.

Olympic, painted light grey for the benefit of press photographers, was launched on 20 October 1910 in front of a crowd of nearly 100,000. The Harland and Wolff workers who had stopped work to be present at the launch were not paid for the time!

After the hull reached the waters of the river Lagan, it was towed to the Thompson Graving Dock, at the time the largest dry dock

Above: Duke of Albany. L & NW Fleetwood–Belfast ferry carried a *Titanic* anchor to Northern Ireland. Sunk in 1916.

Below left: Olympic at Belfast. Her forward funnel was the last to be fitted.

Below right: Photo taken from *Olympic* two days before the launch of *Titanic*, seen here in a distant gantry to the left. (Private collection)

in the world, where fitting-out work commenced with the aid of the 200-ton Benrather crane purchased from Germany.

On the windy and clear 31 May 1911, the hull of *Titanic* took to the water just after 12.15 p.m., and the newly completed *Olympic* departed Belfast, accompanied by the Cherbourg tenders *Nomadic* and *Traffic*, for her maiden voyage. En route to Southampton *Olympic* made a courtesy call at Liverpool on 1 June 1911. On board at the time were J. Pierpont Morgan, Thomas Andrews and J. Bruce Ismay, who, on the maiden voyage, was so delighted with the first vessel that he decided to exercise the option for a third, eventually to be named *Britannic*.

In 1911 and 1912 *Olympic* returned to Belfast for repairs: first between 6 October and 20 November 1911 after her collision with the Royal Navy's cruiser HMS *Hawke*; and, second, from 2–7 March 1912, after she had lost a blade from her port propeller during an eastbound transatlantic crossing. Each time the workers,

Left: *Titanic* takes to the water, 31 May 1911.

Centre left: White Star Line letter heading for SS *Laurentic*, 15 April 1911. *Titanic* sank exactly one year later.

Bottom left: The maiden arrival of *Olympic* in New York. (*Scientific American*)

Below: Advertisement for maiden voyage of *Olympic*, 14 June 1911.

WHITE STAR LINE.

TRIPLE-SCREW STEAMER

"OLYMPIC," 45,000 Tons,

The Largest and Finest Vessel in the World.

This superb steamer, which has unrivaled accommodation, including Dining Saloons, Restaurant, Lounges, Drawing Rooms, Reading Rooms, Smoking Rooms, Veranda Café, Palm Court, Gymnasium, Squash Racquet Court, Turkish Baths, Plunge Bath, etc., etc., will sail from

Southampton & Cherbourg (*via* Queenstown)

to New York on

Wednesday, June 14th, 1911,

returning from New York on

Wednesday, June 28th, 1911,

AND REGULARLY THEREAFTER.

Above: The Vinolia 'Otto' soap advertisement for *Titanic* has become famous but it was not the first! (*Ladies Field*)

Right: Collision between *Olympic* and HMS *Hawke*, 1911. (London Illustrated News Ltd)

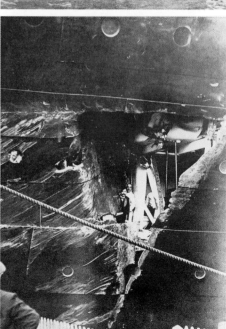

"OLYMPIC" (Triple-Screw), 45,000 Tons.
AND
"TITANIC" (Triple-Screw), 45,000 Tons (Launched May 31st, 1911).
THE LARGEST STEAMERS IN THE WORLD.

SOUTHAMPTON–CHERBOURG–QUEENSTOWN–NEW YORK SERVICE
Calling at QUEENSTOWN (Westbound) and PLYMOUTH (Eastbound).

FROM SOUTHAMPTON.			FROM CHERBOURG.	STEAMER.	FROM NEW YORK. CALLING AT PLYMOUTH AND CHERBOURG.		
Date.	Day.	Sailing hour.	Sailing about 4-30 p.m.		Date.	Day.	Sailing Hour.
1911 Aug. 2	Wed.	Noon	1911 Aug. 2	OCEANIC	1911 Aug.12	Sat.	Noon
... 9	Wed	Noon	... 9	**OLYMPIC**	... 19	Sat.	Noon
... 16	Wed.	Noon	... 16	*ST. PAUL	... 26	Sat	Noon
... 23	Wed.	Noon	... 23	OCEANIC	Sep 2	Sat.	Noon
... 30	Wed.	2-30 pm	... 30	**OLYMPIC**	... 9	Sat.	Noon
Sep 6	Wed.	Noon	Sep. 6	MAJESTIC	... 16	Sat	Noon
... 13	Wed.	Noon	... 13	OCEANIC	... 23	Sat.	Noon
... 20	Wed.	11-0 am	... 20	**OLYMPIC**	... 30	Sat.	Noon
... 27	Wed.	Noon	... 27	MAJESTIC	Oct 7	Sat.	Noon
Oct 4	Wed.	Noon	Oct. 4	OCEANIC	... 14	Sat.	Noon
.. 11	Wed.	Noon	... 11	**OLYMPIC**	... 21	Sat.	Noon
... 18	Wed.	Noon	... 18	MAJESTIC	... 28	Sat.	Noon
... 25	Wed.	Noon	... 25	OCEANIC	Nov. 4	Sat.	Noon
Nov 1	Wed.	2-30 pm	Nov. 1	**OLYMPIC**	... 11	Sat.	Noon
... 8	Wed.	Noon	... 8	MAJESTIC	... 18	Sat.	Noon
... 15	Wed.	Noon	... 15	OCEANIC	... 25	Sat.	Noon
... 22	Wed.	Noon	... 22	*ST. LOUIS	Dec. 2	Sat.	Noon
... 29	Wed.	Noon	... 29	**OLYMPIC**	... 9	Sat.	Noon
Dec 6	Wed.	Noon	Dec. 6	OCEANIC	... 16	Sat.	Noon
... 13	Wed.	Noon	... 13	*PHILADELPHIA	... 23	Sat.	Noon
... 20	Wed.	Noon	... 20	**OLYMPIC**	... 30	Sat.	Noon
... 27	Wed.	Noon	... 27	*ST. PAUL	1912 Jan. 6	Sat.	Noon
1912 Jan 3	Wed.	Noon	1912 Jan. 3	OCEANIC	... 13	Sat.	Noon
... 10	Wed.	Noon	... 10	*PHILADELPHIA	... 20	Sat.	Noon
... 17	Wed.	Noon	... 17	**OLYMPIC**	... 27	Sat.	Noon
... 24	Wed.	Noon	... 24	*ST. PAUL	Feb. 3	Sat.	Noon
... 31	Wed.	Noon	... 31	OCEANIC	... 10	Sat.	Noon
Feb 7	Wed.	Noon	Feb. 7	*PHILADELPHIA	... 17	Sat.	Noon
... 14	Wed.	Noon	... 14	**OLYMPIC**	... 24	Sat.	Noon
... 21	Wed.	Noon	... 21	*ST. PAUL	Mar. 2	Sat.	Noon
... 28	Wed.	Noon	... 28	OCEANIC	... 9	Sat.	Noon
Mar 6	Wed.	Noon	Mar. 6	*ST. LOUIS	... 16	Sat.	Noon
... 13	Wed.	Noon	... 13	**OLYMPIC**	... 23	Sat	Noon
... 20	Wed.	Noon	... 20	**TITANIC**	... 30	Sat.	Noon
... 27	Wed.	Noon	... 27	OCEANIC	Apl. 6	Sat.	Noon
Apl 3	Wed.	Noon	Apl. 3	**OLYMPIC**	... 13	Sat.	Noon
... 10	Wed.	Noon	... 10	**TITANIC**	... 20	Sat.	Noon
... 17	Wed.	Noon	... 17	OCEANIC	... 27	Sat.	Noon
... 24	Wed.	Noon	... 24	**OLYMPIC**	May 4	Sat.	Noon

✴ American Line Steamer

Top left: Olympic, centre, in New York, 1911. (*Scientific American*)

Left: The tug *Vulcan*, her stern shown here, assisting *Olympic* after the collision with HMS *Hawke*. She played a large part in the departure of *Titanic* from Southampton. (Rapp)

Above: White Star Line timetable showing *Titanic* departing Southampton on 20 March 1912, followed by her actual maiden departure on 10 April.

LIST OF FIRST CLASS PASSENGERS

UNITED STATES & ROYAL MAIL

TRIPLE SCREW **S. S. "OLYMPIC"**

From New York to Plymouth, Cherbourg and Southampton

SATURDAY, DECEMBER 9, 1911

Commander, E. J. Smith, R.N.R.

Pursers { H. W. McElroy
C. B. Lancaster

Surgeons { W. F. N. O'Loughlin
J. E. Simpson

Chief Steward, A. Latimer

Aanensen, Mr. Philip S.
Abbott, Mr. Frank
Abrahams, Mr. Neville
Adams, Miss P.
Aitken, Mr. R. M.
Alexander, Mr. Alexander
Alexander, Mrs.
Alexander, Miss Anna M.
and maid
Alexandre, Mrs. J. Joseph
and maid
Amberton, Mrs.
Amy, Mr. Charles
Anthony, Mr. J. S.
Anthony, Mrs.
and maid
Arnold, Mr. J. W.
Antrobus, Mr. Philip
Arbib, Mr. E. J.
Arthur, Mr. J. R.
Audenried, Mr. W. G.

Babcock, Mr. E.
Bach, Mr. William
Bahnson, Capt. J.
Barbey, Mr. H. G.
Barday, Mrs. Maud
Barrett, Mrs. M.

Baruch, Mr. E. R.
Bauer, Mr. R. M.
Bauer, Mrs.
Belgrave, Miss Sybil
Bellhouse, Mr. Vernon
Benavides, Mr. Victor
Secretary Legation of Uruguay
Benavides, Miss
Bennet, Mr. O. G.
Bensinger, Mr. B. E.
Bensinger, Mrs.
Bensinger, Master Robert
Bensinger, Jr., Master B. E.
Blackmore, Miss
Blish, Mr. J. D.
Boerema, Mr. M. W.
Boerema, Mrs.
Boggs, Mr. Gardner
Boggs, Mrs.
Boggs, Mrs. Major
Boileau, Mr. S. H.
Bonbright, Mr. William P.
and valet
Bonbright, Mrs.
Bookwalter, Hon. J. W.
Bookwalter, Mr. F. M.
Bookwalter, Mrs.
Borthwick, Mr. James
Boston, Mr. Harry G.
Bostwick, Mrs. J. A.
and maid
Breaker, Mrs. M.
Burke, Mr. Thomas
Busche, Mr. George V. D.
Busk, Mr. C. W.

THE WORLD'S LARGEST AND FINEST STEAMERS

OLYMPIC

Triple-Screw — Now In Commission — 45,000 Tons

Triple-Screw — Building at Belfast — 45,000 Tons

TITANIC

Top left: *Olympic* at sea in her first year of operation.

Above: This *Cedric* passenger list for June 1911 now advertises *Olympic* in commission and *Titanic* building at Belfast.

Left: An *Olympic* passenger list for her 9 December 1911 New York–Southampton voyage. Smith, McElroy, O'Loughlin and Latimer would all lose their lives the following year.

employed on fitting out *Titanic*, were diverted to *Olympic* in order for her to return as quickly as possible to revenue-earning service. The resulting delay meant that the maiden voyage of *Titanic* was finally advertised as being on 10 April 1912. This voyage had been scheduled for January 1912 then, in the middle of 1911, it was changed to 20 March 1912, and further delay caused a rescheduling to April.

During her first year of service, first-class passengers on *Olympic* complained of spray on the open promenade (A) deck. White Star requested that Harland and Wolff deal with this problem on *Titanic* and, during the last six weeks of fitting out, the forward part of her promenade deck was enclosed with glass screens each measuring 31in x 37in that could be opened by means of a crank. This additional work took nearly three weeks and made the two vessels instantly identifiable. These, and several other alterations made during the latter part of the construction of *Titanic*, resulted in an increase in her gross registered tonnage, now approximately 1,000 tons greater than her sister.

Up to twenty-eight Harland and Wolff men were seriously injured and several had so far been killed on *Titanic*. They were not to be the last.

White Star Line advertisement showing *Olympic* 'now in commission'. *Titanic* 'in service', April 1912.

☆ THE WORLD'S LARGEST AND FINEST STEAMERS ☆

OLYMPIC

Triple-Screw—Now In Commission—45,324 Tons

Triple-Screw—In Service, April, 1912—45,000 Tons

☆ **TITANIC** ☆

Titanic nears completion adjacent to Thompson Dock.

Top: 1 April 1912: strong winds, evidenced by the smoke from her funnels, delayed the trials. (Hurst & Co.)

Above: *Titanic* proceeding to trials in Belfast Lough and the Irish Sea, 2 April 1912.

The fitting out having been completed, she was ready for her sea trials on Monday 1 April 1912. Strong winds that day delayed the trials and they took place early the following day. During the trials, the ship was manned by a crew of eighty and commanded by Captain E.J. Smith. He had been a Royal Naval Reserve captain during the Boer War and still held the Admiralty authority to fly the Blue Ensign, rather than the merchant marine Red Ensign, on ships under his command. Smith, who had taken over from temporary Captain Haddock, had previously commanded the *Olympic*, *Adriatic* and *Baltic*. Haddock then replaced Smith on *Olympic*.

FAREWELL TO BELFAST.
DEPARTURE OF THE LARGEST VESSEL IN THE WORLD,
THE WHITE STAR LINER "TITANIC," 46,328 TONS, APRIL 3rd, 1912.

Apart from Belfast Lough, the trials involved *Titanic* steaming approximately 40 miles south into the Irish Sea. Travelling at 18 knots, both her reciprocating engines were put into reverse and she is believed to have come to a halt in just over three minutes over a distance of 3,000ft.

Titanic returned to Belfast at 6.30 p.m. and the Board of Trade surveyor issued her with a passenger certificate for a year. With Thomas Andrews, and a 'guarantee group' of eight men from Harland and Wolff also on board, she departed for Southampton at 8 p.m. on Tuesday 2 April 1912.

This daylight photograph should probably read 'on trials' rather than 'Farewell to Belfast'. *Titanic* finally departed Belfast at 8 p.m.!

two

MAIDEN DEPARTURE

During Wednesday 3 April, *Titanic* steamed down the Irish Sea towards Southampton, her sister ship *Olympic* having departed that day to begin another transatlantic voyage.

Assisted by tugs, *Titanic* backed into Berth 44 just after midnight on Thursday 4 April. She had carried nearly 100 people for the delivery voyage, comprising officers, crew and Harland and Wolff employees putting the finishing touches to the ship prior to the maiden voyage six days later.

The United Kingdom Miners Federation had called for a strike by its members, over a wage dispute, which had begun in late February 1912, ending on 6 April.

American Line's *St Paul* (1895), 11,629grt, arrived from New York on 3 March and did not sail again until 18 May. She almost certainly berthed in the Empress Dock at Southampton and, it is thought, surrendered her passengers and some of her coal to *Titanic*.

Ships of the IMM had been using Southampton since 1907 and dock space at the port became critical, with many tied up after their voyages had been cancelled due to lack of fuel. As well as White Star's reserve vessels *Majestic* and *Oceanic*, the American Line's *New York*, *Philadelphia*, *St Louis* and *St Paul* were all stranded there when *Titanic* arrived. Several of these vessels surrendered some of their passengers and coal to *Titanic*, which had brought nearly 2,000 tons of coal with her from Belfast, and took on board an additional 4,427 tons contributed partly by the IMM vessels and stocks left behind by *Olympic*. Coaling began almost immediately and the ship was moved about 20ft away from the dockside to facilitate the process.

This dirty and tiresome work was finished by the evening of Friday 5 April; the ship was moved back against her berth, coal dust was cleaned away, and paintwork on her superstructure and funnels was touched up. Allowing for her daily – in port – consumption of approximately 400 tons, *Titanic* would sail on 10 April carrying nearly 6,000 tons of coal.

Captain Edward John Smith, who had brought her from Belfast to Southampton for the maiden voyage, commanded *Titanic*. Born in January 1850, Smith joined the White Star Line in 1880 and it had now become a tradition for him to be in charge of each new White Star vessel for the maiden voyage. Earning a salary of £1,250 per annum and an annual bonus of £200 if his ship was not involved in a collision, this was considerably more than that received by his opposite numbers in the Cunard Line. White Star Line had discontinued the title 'commodore' in 1882 and it was not resurrected until 1922, when Captain Hayes was promoted to command the new *Majestic*.

There is little evidence that this maiden voyage was to be Smith's last before retirement. He would have been 62 when he took *Titanic* out of Southampton and the opposition, Cunard Line, had a retirement age of 60. An article in the *New York Times* of 6 June 1911 stated, 'Captain Smith will retire at the end of the present year to be relieved by Captain Haddock.' It appears that this popular captain's career was extended into 1912 to enable him to command *Titanic* on her maiden voyage.

Below left: Illustration of *Olympic* on a log abstract, 1911.

Below: The reverse of the log abstract, showing Captain Smith in command.

R.M.S."OLYMPIC" ARRIVING AT SOUTHAMPTON.

R. M. S. "OLYMPIC." COMMANDER E. J· SMITH, R.N.R.

NEW YORK TO SOUTHAMPTON VIA PLYMOUTH AND CHERBOURG
VOYAGE NO. 4. EAST, SEPTEMBER 9, 1911.
AMBROSE CHANNEL LIGHT VESSEL ABEAM, SEPTEMBER 9. AT 1,45 P.M. DEPARTURE

DATE	WIND	LAT.	LONG.	MILE	REMARKS.
10	E. & NNW.	41,18	63,49	466	LIGHT E'LY TO NNW. WINDS, SMOOTH SEA
11	NW.	44,11	52,27	532	LIGHT TO FRESH NW.WINDS, SLIGHT SEA
12	NW.	47,19	40,58	516	MOD. NW. WIND TO FRESH NW. GALE, ROUGH SEA
13	NW. & SW.	49,22	28,25	516	MOD. NW. GALE TO STRONG SW. WIND, ROUGH SEA
14	S'LY. & E'LY.	49,50	15,46	493	FRESH S'LY. & STRONG E'LY. WINDS, ROUGH SEA
				451	TO EDDYSTONE LIGHT HOUSE

DISTANCE 2974   AVERAGE SPEED 22.10 KNOTS
ARRIVED 15TH. AT 9,17 A.M. PASSAGE 5 DAYS 14 HOURS 32 MINUTES.

Smith was assisted by a team of three senior and four junior officers. Chief Officer Henry Wilde (b. 1872) had been chief officer on *Olympic* with Smith and, at the last moment, was switched to *Titanic*. It is believed that Wilde was scheduled to captain the laid-up *Oceanic* so reluctantly agreed, on the evening of Tuesday 9 April, to join Smith for the maiden return voyage only. Wilde's addition to the team required Chief Officer William Murdoch (b. 1873, age 39) to be downgraded to first officer; he had also served aboard the *Oceanic* and *Adriatic*. Similarly, First Officer Charles Lightoller (b. 1874) became second officer. Lightoller was a good friend of Murdoch and had been first officer on both *Teutonic* and *Majestic*.

Whilst Murdoch and Lightoller were naturally upset by their demotion, Second Officer David Blair was asked to remain ashore for this voyage. It was not until *Titanic* had departed that Blair realised the lookout's binoculars had been placed in a locker in the crow's nest and the key to that locker was in his pocket.

Third Officer Herbert Pitman (b. 1877) had joined White Star in 1906 and was viewed by the company as an up-and-coming employee.

Fourth Officer Joseph Boxhall had joined White Star in 1907 and was particularly adept navigationally.

Fifth Officer Harold Lowe had been with the company for a year and this was to be his first transatlantic crossing.

Sixth Officer James Moody, the youngest, had also been with the company for a year and had transferred from *Oceanic*.

In addition, there were Chief Purser Herbert McElroy, assisted by Mr R.L. Barber, Surgeon William O'Loughlin, assisted by Mr J. Simpson, and Chief Steward A. Latimer.

When *Olympic* departed Southampton she left behind about 250 members of her crew to join *Titanic* for the maiden voyage.

After coaling had finished on Good Friday, 5 April, it was time to recruit the balance of the crew. This began on Saturday 6 April and a considerable number of would-be recruits enlisted, many from the thousands stranded ashore because of the coal strike and grateful for the opportunity to work again. Nearly 900 were employed, including those who had switched from *Olympic*. Most were signed up at the Southampton offices of the British Seafarers' Union.

COAL MINERS' STRIKE, 1912

In 1894 the Miners' Federation of Great Britain, being the predominant union representing Britain's coal miners, staged an unsuccessful strike in demand of a minimum wage. The 1912 strike was the first national strike with the same demands. At the time the negotiated structure was such that it was very hard for a miner to earn a fair wage. The dissatisfaction had started the previous year in South Wales, and had simmered until the beginnings of the national strike in Derbyshire at the end of February 1912. Involving nearly a million men, the strike lasted thirty-seven days and only ended on 6 April, after an intervention by the UK government. The Coal Mines (Minimum Wage) Act 1912 resulted in fairer wages for the miners, but not before shipping and railway schedules had been severely affected.

On Easter Sunday, 7 April, *Titanic* lay quietly alongside her berth prior to the hectic three days preceding her departure. Unlike her sister *Olympic* there had been no public visits to the ship.

On Wednesday 10 April, the London and South Western Railway, owners of the Southampton Docks complex, ran two boat trains from London's Waterloo Station, Platform 12. The first, carrying second- and third-class passengers, was scheduled to depart at 8.30 a.m. and arrive shipside at approximately 10.05 a.m. Second-class passengers could, subject to space, utilise the first-class train that left at 9.45 a.m. and arrived at the dock at approximately 11.20 a.m. The rail fare for the 80-mile journey on the boat train was 11s for first class, 7s for second class and 6s for third class.

First class could embark no later than noon, second class no later than 11 a.m. and third class no later than 10.30 a.m.

The day dawned to reveal a slightly overcast sky and the temperature was to reach 48°F. Early that morning Smith arrived from his home in Southampton, his officers having spent the night aboard. Shortly afterwards the crew were gathered together for inspection. Captain Maurice Clarke, the Board of Trade Immigration Officer, arrived early that morning to observe the crew inspection and witness the lowering of two of the rear starboard lifeboats, the port side being against the dock. Lowe and Moody were designated to supervise the test – the only lifeboat drill ever carried out.

Across the water the two officers observed the liners *St Louis*, *Philadelphia* and *Majestic* moored side by side and looking tiny in comparison to their own giant vessel.

Thomas Andrews had written to his wife the previous night: 'The Titanic is now about complete and will, I think, do the old firm credit tomorrow when we sail.' He had arrived on board very early that morning.

White Star Line's chairman and managing director, J. Bruce Ismay, with wife Julia and three of his children, came aboard at 9.30 that morning. His family did not travel but his valet and secretary accompanied him.

Top left: Boat train Platform 12 at Waterloo Station. (Kingsway)

Top right: The railway lines to the docks are clearly visible in this aerial view of the South Western Hotel and Docks Station, Southampton. (Photochrom Co. Ltd / private collection)

Above: L&SWR Docks Station, Southampton. (CPC London / private collection)

Titanic at Berth 44 in the White Star Dock at Southampton prior to her maiden departure.

Majestic, *Philadelphia* and *St Louis* at Berth 46 opposite the White Star Dock. The stern of *Titanic* is visible to the right. The postcard was produced by amateur photographer Herbert Willsteed, who worked as a baggage handler for Royal Mail Lines in Southampton. (Willsteed / private collection)

American Line's *St Louis* (1895), 11,629grt, arrived from New York on 24 March and berthed outboard of *Philadelphia* at Berth 46 in the White Star Dock.

American Line's *Philadelphia* (1889), 10,669grt, originally Inman Line's *City of Paris* and sister to *New York*, arrived at Southampton from New York on 4 February and tied up to White Star's *Majestic* at Berth 46. She departed on 1 May with the hastily rescheduled White Star sailing to New York.

White Star's *Majestic* (1890), 9,965grt, originally built with three masts and designed by Carlisle. She was a reserve vessel at Southampton as *Titanic* departed and was brought back into service after the disaster. (Priestley & Co.)

SOUTH WESTERN HOTEL, SOUTHAMPTON.

South Western Hotel, Southampton. Both Ismay and Andrews stayed here prior to the maiden departure of *Titanic*. (*Daily News*)

Titanic would have appeared much the same in this view, probably from the South Western Hotel, of *Olympic* in the White Star Dock. (F.G.O. Stuart)

The port side of *Olympic* against Berth 44 in the White Star Dock. The view of *Titanic* would have been the same.

One of the visitors to the ship that morning was artist Norman Wilkinson, responsible for the paintings in the first-class smoking rooms of the two liners: 'The Approach to the New World' on *Olympic* and 'Plymouth Harbour' on *Titanic*. Wilkinson had been given a guided tour by one of the pursers.

As the time of departure drew near, the scene at Berth 44 became more hectic. The passengers were boarded through separate class entrances. Third-class passengers were checked for the eye disease trachoma, as sufferers were not allowed entry into the USA. At least one man was denied boarding. Over half of the third-class passengers did not speak English as their native language.

Just after 12 noon the whistles on the first two funnels sounded. Wilde and Lightoller were both on the forecastle supervising the release of the bow mooring lines, and Murdoch and Pitman dealt with the stern lines. Boxhall and Lowe were stationed in the bridge area, and Moody was in charge of the last remaining gangway on E deck that linked the ship to the dockside.

As members of the ship's band played on deck, the two outer propellers of *Titanic* began to turn. Assisted by the tugs *Vulcan*, *Ajax*, *Hercules*, *Neptune*, *Albert Edward* and *Hector*, Southampton pilot Mr George Bowyer supervised the left turn into

Southampton Water. Bowyer was a favourite of the White Star Line and had been on board *Olympic* for her maiden voyage the previous year. He did not refer to *Titanic* in his memoirs.

Proceeding down Southampton Water at a speed of 6 knots, *Titanic* drew parallel on her port side with the liners *Oceanic* inside and *New York* outside, moored together at Berth 39. Her displacement and the power of her propellers created suction that caused the lines holding *New York* to break and the vessel began to drift slowly towards *Titanic*. Captain Smith and Pilot George Bowyer stopped the engines; Captain Gale of the tug *Vulcan* secured a line to *New York* and began to drag his charge away from the stationary *Titanic*. At one point the two hulls were only 4ft apart. Two tugs then pulled *New York* away and she was secured at the edge of the Eastern Docks in the river Itchen.

Titanic restarted her engines and, before dropping off the pilot at the *Nab* light vessel, stopped as the tug *Vulcan* on the port side collected any crew surplus to requirements for the maiden crossing. This contributed, along with the *New York* incident, to a late

Left: A close-up view of *Titanic* as she departed Southampton featured on French sheet music, *Plus Pres de Toi mon Dieu* (*Nearer my God to Thee*).

Below: White Star Line's *Oceanic* (1899), 17,274grt, arrived from New York on 17 March under the command of Captain Haddock, who left her to assume command of *Titanic* in Belfast. She was scheduled to take the Wednesday White Star sailing to New York on 17 April but, under the circumstances, this voyage appears to have been cancelled. She was tied up at Berth 39 until 8 May, when she departed for New York. (Priestley & Co.)

En souvenir du vaisseau "TITANIC" et des vaillants qui ont péri le 15 Avril 1912.

PLUS PRÈS DE TOI MON DIEU !

(NEARER MY GOD TO THEE!)

Hymne exécuté à bord, la nuit, au moment du naufrage

PAROLES (FRANÇAISES ET ANGLAISES) ET MUSIQUE AUTHENTIQUES

Petit format : 0 35   LE TITANIC   Grand format, net : 1 fr.

Henry WYKES, éditeur, 166, Rue Montmartre — PARIS

TOUS DROITS RÉSERVÉS

American Line's *New York* (1888), 10,499grt, originally Inman Line's *City of New York*, arrived on 10 March from New York. On 10 April she was moored outboard of *Oceanic* at Berth 39. The suction from *Titanic* caused her to snap her moorings and drift towards the giant liner. The tug *Vulcan*, assisting *Titanic*, took her in tow and she was finally secured against Berth 37. She departed for New York on 11 May.

Royal Mail Steam Packet Company's *Tagus* (1899), 5,545grt, departed on 10 April at 12.55 p.m. for the West Indies. She followed *Titanic* out of Southampton but, with a shallower draft, took the western route round the Isle of Wight.

VULCAN

The tugboat *Vulcan*, owned by the Southampton, Isle of Wight and South of England Royal Mail Steam Packet Ltd Company (Red Funnel Line), was built in Glasgow in 1893 by Barclay, Curle & Co. Ltd. With a gross tonnage of 288, this twin-screw vessel first came to the attention of the public when she provided assistance to *Titanic*'s sister ship, RMS *Olympic*, at the time of the collision between *Olympic* and the Royal Navy's cruiser HMS *Hawke* in 1911. In April of the following year she was one of six tugs that assisted *Titanic* at the time of her departure from Southampton. Under the command of Captain Gale, *Vulcan* was one of the two tugs that helped draw the liner SS *New York* away from *Titanic*, thus preventing the near collision, after *New York* snapped her mooring lines and began to drift into the path of the White Star liner. Once *New York* had been secured, *Vulcan* then drew alongside *Titanic*'s port quarter and removed the remaining standby crewmen who had not disembarked at Berth 44.

Vulcan was broken up at Milford Haven in 1927.

Above: Sheet music *Be British* featuring *Titanic* with tug *Vulcan* alongside taking off surplus crew in Southampton Water.

Top right: *Titanic* proceeds down Southampton Water towards Cherbourg.

Right: *Titanic* approaches the Isle of Wight with ferry *Lord Kitchener* on the right. (Private collection)

Lord Kitchener at Bembridge, Isle of Wight. She ferried passengers from here and Seaview to the mainland. (Kingsway / private collection)

arrival at Cherbourg. She then proceeded towards the Isle of Wight as passengers began to explore their new home. It is estimated that on leaving Southampton the ship was carrying 1,842 people.

Captain Smith, in an interview with the *New York Times* whilst in command of *Adriatic* in 1907, is quoted as saying:

Shipbuilding is such a perfect art nowadays that absolute disaster involving the passengers is inconceivable. Whatever happens, there will be time enough before the vessel sinks to save the life of every person on board. I will go a bit further. I will say that I cannot imagine any condition that would cause the vessel to founder. Modern shipbuilding has gone beyond that!

three

PORTS OF CALL

*T*itanic turned left into the eastern route and rounded the Isle of Wight. The more obvious route to Cherbourg would have required her to take the western passage, but there had been insufficient dredging to allow her to pass through

Having left Southampton at around 1.15 p.m. on Wednesday 10 April, she steamed 90 miles across the English Channel and arrived at Cherbourg as the sun was setting at about 6.30 p.m.

Twenty cross-Channel passengers prepared to leave the ship, thirteen in first class, who had each paid £1 10s, and seven in second class, who had paid £1. Those passengers travelling on to Queenstown paid £4

Titanic passing Ryde Pier, Isle of Wight, on her way to Cherbourg. (W.R. Hogg)

The White Star Triple Liner "Titanic", 45,000 Tons, passing Ryde Pier April 10th, 1912. Sank with 1,535 people off Newfoundland, April 15th, 1912.

in first and £3 in second class. Queenstown passengers could only be booked from Southampton if those bound for the USA had not taken all the berths, a situation that often occurred in the busy autumn period.

White Star Line was keen to promote their cross-Channel services and their advertising material stated:

These steamers carry passengers between Southampton, Cherbourg and Queenstown which includes an excellent table and all necessities. This makes one of the most comfortable routes to and from France and England and is also the shortest and best route to the south of Ireland.

Titanic anchored in the Rade at about 6.30 p.m., as the first sitting dinner was announced, and awaited the arrival of the tenders *Nomadic* and *Traffic*.

That morning in Paris at the Gare Saint-Lazare, the *Train Transatlantique* was preparing to depart at 9.40 a.m. with her passengers for *Titanic*. The advertised costs for this journey were: first class 34s 3d ($8.56), second class 23s 7d ($5.90) and third class 15s 11d ($4.10). The journey to Cherbourg's Gare Maritime was scheduled to take just over six hours. Tender embarkation, scheduled for 4.30 p.m., had been delayed by an hour due to the late arrival.

Most of the newly arrived passengers had taken the train from Paris and they then spent the next uncomfortable hour in the small Gare Maritime until boarding the tenders at 5.30 p.m., both of which

The Gare Saint-Lazare, Paris, from where the boat train for *Titanic* transported many of her passengers to Cherbourg.

LES GRANDS TRAINS FRANÇAIS
II   Chemins de fer de l'Etat.
Train transatlantique Paris-Cherbourg. — ND. Phot.

CHERBOURG   La Gare Maritime, Vue extérieure

6. CHERBOURG — Gare Maritime

Col. Emile Dupont, CJ.

Above left: The *Train Transatlantique*. Train No. 317 was scheduled to depart at 9.52 a.m. and arrive approximately six hours later carrying all three classes of passengers. (ND / private collection)

Above right: The old Gare Maritime at Cherbourg. Having disembarked the train from Paris, passengers passed through here to the tenders. (Ratti)

Left: The other side of the Gare Maritime and tenders, with probably the stern of *Traffic* in the foreground, waiting to take passengers out to the liner anchored in the Rade. (Emile Dupont / private collection)

39

The old White Star tender *Gallic*, replaced in 1911 by *Nomadic* and *Traffic*. (ND)

216 CHERBOURG. — *Départ du Transbordeur « Gallic ».* — **ND** *Phot.*

The tenders *Traffic* and *Nomadic* return to port at Cherbourg. (LL)

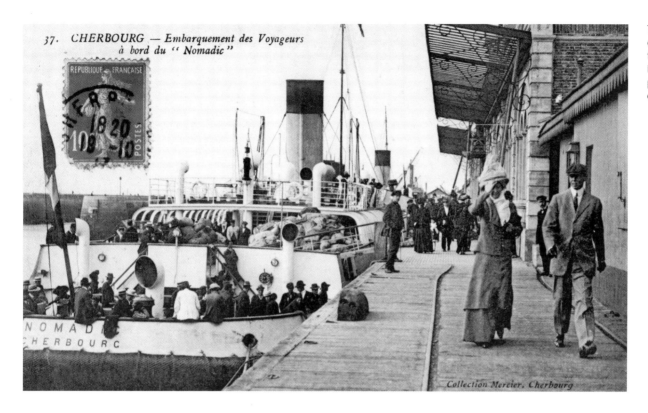

37. CHERBOURG — *Embarquement des Voyageurs à bord du " Nomadic "*

Collection Mercier, Cherbourg

The stern of *Nomadic*, with quite possibly *Traffic* in front, at the Gare Maritime. Notice the French custom at the time of putting the stamp on the front of the postcard. (Mercier)

CHERBOURG TENDER *NOMADIC*

Nomadic was built at Harland and Wolff, Belfast, in 1911, primarily to act as a Cherbourg tender to the Olympic-class liners. The 1,273grt *Nomadic* was designed to carry approximately 1,000 passengers, and their baggage, in first and second classes. The International Mercantile Marine Company sold *Nomadic*, in 1927, to Compagnie Cherbourgeoise de Transbordement of Paris, but she continued to service White Star Line vessels. After the merger with the Cunard Line in 1934, *Nomadic* was sold to Société Cherbourgeoise de Sauvetage et de Remorquage (SCSR) and renamed *Ingenieur Minard*, her White Star Line funnel colours being replaced by black with a red band.

At the time of the German invasion of France in 1940, *Ingenieur Minard* assisted in the evacuation of British forces from Le Havre and escaped to the UK. Throughout the war she acted primarily as a minelayer and patrol vessel along the south coast of England. After the war, *Ingenieur Minard* resumed her tender duties at Cherbourg until 1968. Renamed *Nomadic*, the vessel served as a floating restaurant in Paris on the river Seine from 1974 until 1999. In 2003 she was towed to Le Havre and sold to the Department of Social Development of the Northern Ireland Government for £250,001 – £1 above the reserve price. She was towed back to Belfast, arriving on 17 July 2006, and has now been almost fully restored there as the only surviving Harland and Wolff-built White Star Line vessel.

CHERBOURG TENDER *TRAFFIC*

Also built at Harland and Wolff, Belfast, in 1911, as a Cherbourg tender, the 675grt *Traffic* was to be primarily a back-up vessel to her near sister *Nomadic*. She would normally transfer third-class passengers and baggage. As with her sister *Nomadic*, she was sold in 1927 and again in 1934, when she was renamed *Ingenieur Riebell*.

She was scuttled by the French at Cherbourg in June 1940 but was raised by the occupying German forces. In January 1941, whilst in German naval service, she was sunk in action in the English Channel.

departed filled to less than a quarter capacity. First to arrive alongside was *Traffic*, bringing the mail and 102 third-class passengers. *Nomadic* arrived at about 7 p.m. with her first- and second-class, primarily American, passengers.

The liner was fitted with gangways but those on the two tenders were employed that evening and, owing to the swell in the harbour, were held steady by the crew.

The 142 first- and 30 second-class passengers from *Nomadic* embarked into the D-deck entrance and reception room. *Traffic* returned with the disembarking cross-Channel passengers.

At 8.10 p.m., *Titanic* departed for the overnight journey to Queenstown, Ireland.

Thomas Andrews wrote again to his wife, posting the letter the next day:

Lights blazing, a heavily retouched *Titanic* departs Cherbourg for the overnight journey to Queenstown. (PB)

We reached here in nice time and took on board quite a number of passengers. The two little tenders looked well, you will remember we built them about a year ago. We expect to arrive at Queenstown about 10.30am tomorrow. The weather is fine and everything shaping for a good voyage.

The overnight journey took fourteen hours in calm seas at a speed of nearly 21 knots, using twenty of the ship's twenty-nine boilers. She dropped anchor 2 miles offshore at 11.30 a.m. on Thursday 11 April as the first of the two tenders, *America*, was approaching. *America* manoeuvred against the liner's port side and began disembarking her passengers through a gangway door on E deck. Meanwhile, the second tender, *Ireland*, came along the starboard side to disembark her passengers. The two tenders had made the thirty-minute journey from Scott's Quay to *Titanic* in beautiful sunshine carrying 3 first-class, 7 second-class and 113 third-class emigrant passengers, as well as 1,385 sacks of mail. Dominating the Queenstown skyline was the cathedral of St Coleman nearing completion, whose tall spire would eventually be added in 1914.

The railway station at Queenstown. Passengers arriving here would then proceed up the hill to the tenders *America* and *Ireland* waiting at the wharf. (Stewart & Woolf / private collection)

At the White Star Wharf Queenstown.

The White Star Wharf at Queenstown. The cathedral spire was added in 1914. (Fergus O'Connor)

TENDERS AT QUEENSTOWN

The 240-ton paddle steamers *Ireland* and *America*, built in 1891, registered in Glasgow and owned by the Clyde Shipping Company, tendered the various White Star Line vessels that came through the port of Queenstown (now Cobh), Ireland.

On Thursday 11 April 1912, *Ireland* departed Scott's Quay carrying three first-class and seven second-class passengers, and proceeded to the Deepwater Quay, where she began taking on 1,385 sacks of mail for the United States. Her sister *America*, carrying the 113 third-class passengers and their baggage, soon joined her. Both vessels then transported their passengers, only forty-four of whom were to survive, and mail out to the waiting *Titanic*.

In the autumn of 1915 both vessels were commissioned as naval rescue tugs, often being called to the assistance of ships torpedoed off the Southern Irish coast. *America* continued in this capacity to the end of the First World War, but *Ireland* was later converted into a minelayer.

Both vessels resumed their tendering duties after the end of the war. In March 1928 they were offered for sale and, two months later, transferred to a Belgian company.

The tenders returned to Scott's Quay with seven first-class passengers and a considerable amount of mail. One member of the crew, fireman John Caffey, had secretly deserted the ship.

Titanic departed Queenstown at 1.30 p.m., the US flag flying from her mainmast. She dropped her pilot and began working up to a speed of nearly 21 knots. By 2.30 p.m. she was 3 miles off the Old Head of Kinsale and, after reaching the Fastnet light by about 4.30 p.m., she headed out into the North Atlantic towards New York. It is estimated she was carrying 2,208 souls: 324 first-class, 284 second-class, 709 third-class passengers and a crew of 891.

White Star Line captains had received a letter from their company stating:

> You are to dismiss all ideas of competitive passages with other vessels and to concentrate your attention upon a cautious, prudent and ever watchful system of navigation, which shall lose time or suffer any other temporary inconvenience rather than incur the slightest risk which can be avoided.

One of the many letters mailed at Queenstown on 11 April 1912 was from Chief Officer Wilde to his sister, in which he wrote, 'I still don't like this ship … I have a queer feeling about it.'

four

LIFE AT SEA

Second-class passenger Lawrence Beesley wrote, 'There is very little to relate from the time of leaving Queenstown on Thursday to Sunday morning. The sea was calm.' Allowing for the subsequent events of the voyage, this was probably the case but, given the fact that over 2,200 people lived together for more than three days, it is worth looking further into their lives and duties over this period.

On board the delivery voyage from Belfast to Southampton were Captain Smith, his officers and a crew of approximately sixty with a few invited dignitaries.

A menu from that journey, dated 2 April, offered such delicacies as consomme mirrette (a clear soup with mushrooms), sweetbreads, bovin potatoes (boiled in beef broth), golden plover on toast and pudding sans souci, in addition to a considerable number of less glamorous items.

The boat deck, accommodating the officers' quarters, gymnasium and compass platform, was primarily the promenade areas for officers, first-class passengers, engineers and second-class passengers, forward to aft. On the deck below, referred to as the promenade A deck, were the first-class public rooms: lounge, reading and writing room, smoking room and Verandah (Palm Court) Café.

Olympic was often shown as *Titanic* on postcards, as evidenced here by the open first-class promenade deck.

Titanic correctly shown here but with 'added' smoke pouring from the rear funnel, which was a dummy for kitchen exhaust and engine room ventilation.

The more expensive first-class cabins, including two Promenade suites, were located on B deck, as was the first-class B Deck Restaurant, on the starboard side of which was the innovative Café Parisien, the second-class smoking room and a second-class promenade.

Many more first-class cabins were located on C deck, in addition to the barber shop, purser's and enquiry offices, telephone exchange, maids' and valets' saloon, and second-class lounge, on either side of which were more promenades. Further aft, in the poop section of C deck, were the third-class general and smoking rooms. Separating the main superstructure and poop areas was the aft well deck, used as a third-class promenade.

The main first- and second-class (situated aft) dining rooms were located on D deck, often referred to as the saloon deck. These restaurants extended to each side of the ship and were separated by a galley that served both. In addition to cabins for all three classes, D deck also featured a forward well-deck promenade for third-class passengers. Shipping law in 1912 required that third-class (steerage) open deck space not be more than two decks above interior accommodation, hence the frequent use of forward and aft well decks for third-class promenade areas. Far forward, in the bow on D deck, the nearly 200 firemen were accommodated in two large dormitories.

E deck was the lowest deck to offer first-class cabins, but featured accommodation for all three classes, as well as, on the port side, for the crew, including stewards in the first and second classes, waiters, cooks and the ship's orchestra. The portside alleyway, often referred to as 'Scotland Road', provided third-class passengers and the crew the means of getting from one end of the ship to the other.

The third-class dining room and kitchen, in addition to second- and third-class cabins and engineers' accommodation, were all located on F deck.

G deck was divided fore and aft by the two engines and boilers. The baggage storage areas and mailroom were situated in the forward section.

On board the new White Star "Olympic"

COLMAN'S
D.S.F. MUSTARD

The Louis XIV. Restaurant on the New White Star Atlantic Liner "Olympic."
Colman's D.S.F. Mustard is being exclusively used on this magnificent
floating palace.
It is here, as always, the finishing touch to the perfectly served meal.

Left This Colman's Mustard advertisement features the B-deck restaurant on the maiden departure of *Olympic*. (Illustrated London News Ltd)

Left: A first-class menu from the maiden voyage of *Olympic* in 1911.

Below: By 1912 the choices were greater. 'Blue Points' are a type of oyster.

R.M.S. "OLYMPIC."

JUNE 18, 1911.

HORS D'ŒUVRES VARIES

CONSAMMÉ OLGA
CRÈME À L'OLYMPIC

BRILL, SHRIMP SAUCE

FILLET OF BEEF & MUSHROOMS
VOL AU VENT, TOULOUSE

BAKED VIRGINIA HAM À L'AMERICAINE

SIRLOIN OF BEEF, CHATEAU POTATOES
LAMB, MINT SAUCE
ROAST SURREY CAPON

GREEN PEAS   ASPARAGUS
BOILED RICE
BOILED NEW POTATOES

SPAGHETTI AU SUGA

PÂTÉ DE FOIE GRAS
SALAD

PUDDING À LA FEDORA
RHUBARB TART & WHIPPED CREAM
GENOESE SLICES   WINE JELLY

FRENCH ICE CREAM

R.M.S. "OLYMPIC."

JANUARY 28. 1912

HORS D'ŒUVRE VARIÉS
BLUE POINTS

CONSOMMÉ DUBORG   CHICKEN GUMBO

SALMON TROUT, SAUCE MOUSSELINE

CHICKEN SAUTÉ, MARINGO
LAMB CUTLETS, ANGELIQUE

SIRLOIN OF BEEF, HORSERADISH CREAM
TURKEY. CRANBERRY SAUCE
BRAISED VIRGINIA HAM À L'AMERICAINE

BRUSSELS SPROUTS   EGG PLANT
BOILED RICE
CREAMED & BOILED POTATOES

PUNCH ROMAINE

TEAL DUCK, PORT WINE SAUCE
COLD ASPARAGUS VINAIGRETTE
PÂTÉ DE FOIE GRAS
CELERY

PUDDING ROYALE
PEACHES IN CHARTREUSE JELLY
PETIT FOURS

FRENCH ICE CREAM

On boarding, first- and second-class passengers were given the choice of elevator or stairs to reach their cabins. *Titanic* was equipped with three elevators in first class that operated as far down as E deck. Alternatively, passengers in first class could use the forward staircase, descending as far as F deck, no known photographs of which exist. There were two staircases serving the first-class decks; often named 'grand staircases', neither the builder nor owners used this expression. A large glass and wrought-iron dome, illuminated at night, covered each.

First class was positioned solely amidships from the boat deck down to E deck. Those cabins in the forward part of B deck were generally accepted as being the most prominent, having been added at a later stage of the vessel's construction, after it was decided to remove the planned B-deck promenade. Many of these cabins could quickly be converted into suites if necessary and benefited from windows rather than portholes.

The two Promenade suites each had a 50ft expanse of private deck and comprised three cabin areas. Bruce Ismay travelled free in one, while Mrs Charlotte Cardeza and her son, paying £512 6s, occupied the second. Other than these two suites, very few of the first-class cabins had private bathrooms.

Having boarded, many of the passengers took the opportunity to explore their surroundings. Some would have gone straight to the luxurious reception room on D deck prior to entering the dining room for lunch, and gentlemen may have visited the smoking room, furnished with a large fireplace over which hung Norman Wilkinson's painting of Plymouth Harbour. This room, with small tables, high ceiling and dark furniture, was predominantly a male enclave, whereas the ladies favoured the reading and writing room. This delightful room, with an 'Old Rose'-coloured carpet and high ceiling that extended partially up to the boat deck, was open from 8 a.m. to 11.30 p.m. and featured a bookcase stocked by the Times Book Club. This room, like the smoking room, offered a fireplace and would also have been reached by an oak-panelled passageway. Both the elevators and the forward staircase led to the first-class boat deck entrance featuring a linoleum floor and six electric heaters. Many of the external public rooms on the upper decks had revolving doors to counteract the outside draughts.

Passengers with dogs – it is thought that more than ten dogs boarded at Southampton – proceeded to the kennels located on the starboard side of F deck, just aft of amidships.

In addition to these sedate activities, first-class passengers on *Titanic* could indulge in slightly more active pastimes.

The swimming pool on F deck, measuring 32ft x 13ft with a depth of 6ft, was filled with heated saltwater. Tickets for the pool, purchased from the enquiry office on C deck at a charge of 1*s* (25¢), also included the use of a costume. Gentlemen were free to use the pool from 6 a.m. to 9 a.m. and ladies from 10 a.m. to noon, but both would be charged at all other times. A swimming pool was a complete luxury at sea in 1912 and was almost unique to White Star's Olympic-class vessels.

To use the adjacent Turkish baths, the charge was 4*s* ($1) and tickets were also purchased at the enquiry office; this charge included use of the swimming pool.

White Star Line advertised:

○———————————————○

TURKISH, ELECTRIC AND SWIMMING BATHS

A fully equipped Turkish bath is situated on Deck F, consisting of the usual steam, hot, temperate, shampooing and cooling rooms. Electric baths and a Swimming Bath are also provided in conjunction with same, and experienced attendants will be in charge.

Also on F, and G (for height), deck was the squash racquet court. Use of this facility was charged at 2*s* (50¢) per half an hour. White Star Line advertising stated that the professional in attendance (Fred Wright on *Titanic*) was authorised to sell and hire balls and racquets. This court could be reserved in advance, upon application to the professional in charge, and could not be occupied for longer than one hour at a time if others were waiting. The court was so popular, on *Olympic*, that it was decided to reduce this hour to thirty minutes.

White Star Line advertising again:

○———————————————○

A GYMNASIUM, fully supplied with modern appliances, is situated on the Boat Deck and is open for exercise by Ladies and Gentlemen during the same hours as the Baths, no charge being made for the use of the appliances. The Gymnasium will be available for Children from 1 to 3pm only.

The gymnasium steward on *Titanic*, T.W. McCawley, has been referred to as a 'sturdy little man in white flannels'.

Second-class passengers were almost of an equal mix of British and American, and their accommodation would have matched first class on many other vessels. Not offered the facilities of first class, their comforts nevertheless included a lounge and oak-panelled smoking room as well as ample promenades. Boat deck and B deck featured open promenades with sheltered areas on C deck. Second-class accommodation was primarily located in the aft section of amidships and, as with all White Star Line passengers, the occupants were asked not to stray into first or third-class quarters.

THE LARGEST STEAMER IN THE WORLD

THE TRIPLE SCREW

"OLYMPIC"

WHITE STAR LINE

SOME VIEWS IN THE SECOND CLASS

With much talk of millionaires and emigrants, it is worth noting that *Titanic* did also carry second-class passengers. Details, rarely shown, of second-class accommodation on *Olympic*, and thus *Titanic* also, in this White Star Line booklet.

The second-class promenade area at the rear of *Olympic*'s boat deck.

Above: The *Olympic* second-class stairway from the boat deck to A deck. Note the main (rear) mast by the piano.

Above right: The *Olympic* second-class promenade on B deck. Note the neatly folded steamer chairs.

Right: The *Olympic* second-class stairway on B deck showing the one elevator in second class.

Above left: *Olympic*'s ornate second-class dining room with swivel chairs facing outwards for the photographer.

Above right: *Olympic*'s second-class lounge, often referred to as the Library, was popular with the ladies.

Left: *Olympic*'s second-class smoking room: a male enclave.

Above: Note the double washbasins in this four-berth cabin in *Olympic*'s second class.

Above right: A remarkably uncluttered two-berth cabin in second class aboard *Olympic*.

Second-class passengers boarding through an entrance on B deck, pierced by the aft (main) mast, were greeted by the innovative elevator, running from boat to F deck, and spacious cabins occupying the full width of the ship, located on decks D, E, F and G. The cabins did not have private bathrooms so occupants were required to use the public bathrooms on D deck, but each had a washbasin and chamberpot. Heating was provided by a hot-air system that later proved to be problematical.

The second-class smoking room, again a predominantly male enclave, located aft on B deck, was surrounded by an open promenade area. Directly below, on C deck, was the second-class lounge, often referred to as the Library, the six windows on each side of which overlooked a covered promenade.

Prior to 1912 the White Star Line dropped the word 'steerage' from company advertising, replacing it with 'third class'. The spacious living conditions in third class matched second class in many other vessels, and the accommodation was usually superior to that which passengers were accustomed. *Titanic* carried over 700 passengers in third class, most of whom were immigrating to the USA and less than half spoke English as their native language, including those from Ireland. Around 200 came from Sweden, Norway and Finland. In addition to Russians, Bulgarians and Syrians were eight Chinese en route to join another ship in New York. There was space for almost a thousand in third class. Passengers were, of necessity, forced to use narrow corridors to access their accommodation. Generally embarkation for third class took place earlier than other classes because the processing of so many multinational people presented more problems than usual.

White Star Line had a policy of berthing the single men, from age 14, forward in third class and the single women, married couples and families aft. A limited number of two- and four-berth cabins in third class had washbasins so the company suggested early booking in order to secure such accommodation. The majority of the third-class cabins were two-, four- or six-berth and all were well ventilated and lit by electricity. The beds featured the White Star Line red and white coverlet but the single men forward were only allocated mattresses, blankets and pillows, and were required to provide their own sheets and pillowcases.

Open deck promenade areas in third class were on the forward well deck, in good weather, and the aft well deck and stern (poop) deck, beneath which were the two main third-class public areas. The general room proved a popular meeting place for families. Framed in pine with white enamel walls, it was furnished with teak furniture and featured a well-used upright piano. Third-class passengers generally provided their own entertainment.

Adjacent to the general room was the third-class smoking room. Located on the port side of the stern C deck, this room was, like its first- and second-class counterparts, primarily used by the men. Smoking indoors was frowned upon in those days unless one was in a smoking room, and the habit was considered to be very unladylike. The popular smoking room, oak panelled with teak furniture and patterned linoleum, was served by one bar, which also catered to the general room.

US immigration laws required shipping companies to adopt a policy of strict segregation between cabin (first- and second-class) and steerage (third-class) passengers. Upon arrival in New York steerage passengers were disembarked and processed on Ellis Island, the vessel proceeding to her company's pier and disembarking her cabin passengers. One means of segregation was the installation of internal lockable gates, and these had been fitted on *Titanic*. This was a US immigration requirement to prevent the possibility of third-class passengers infecting their travelling companions in other classes. In the event of any sickness being newly detected on board, there was a third-class surgery located on D deck amidships aft. There were no circumstances under which a third-class passenger was allowed in another class either in White Star regulations or under 1912 social situations. Third-class passengers had easy access to their own open deck areas in which, externally at least, there were only small gates and signs in English to dissuade them from joining their fellow travellers. However, during the voyage, third class would have familiarised themselves with their own areas and would have given scant interest to what lay above; however, there is reason to believe that, on the night of the disaster, internal locked gates did confront some third-class passengers.

It is often thought that all classes were invited to join the captain in first class for the Divine Service on Sunday. This was not the case: separate services were held in the respective classes. White Star Line advertising stated: 'First class passengers are not allowed to enter Second or Third class compartments, or vice versa, as complications might arise under the Quarantine Regulations.'

The company discouraged contact between crew and passengers, so the crew's mess and dormitory accommodation were kept completely separate. Sailors and firemen were housed in dormitories in the forecastle on D, E, F and G decks and would eat in C deck above. The firemen's quarters on D deck accommodated fifty-four berths to allow for each watch of four hours, and the boiler rooms, which could often reach 120°F, were accessed by a spiral staircase. The waiters, stewards (separated by class), bakers etc. all had separate accommodation primarily on E deck and the eighteen stewardesses were housed in three cabins amongst the passengers on higher decks.

The engineers' mess was also located on E deck, their cabins one deck below and their promenade area between the first- and second-class promenade sections on the boat deck.

Seamen and firemen received £5 per month. Male stewards were paid £3 15s per month, whereas their female counterparts received 5s per month less, the income of stewards, stewardesses and waiters being supplemented by tips. The thirty-five first-class bedroom stewards each took care of five bedrooms or fewer, the twelve in second class up to ten cabins and the forty-four stewards in third class would each take care of twenty-five or more cabins. The six lookouts operating three two-man shifts, two hours on and four off, were paid £5 5s per month, 5s more than an able seaman. A Turkish bath stewardess received £4 per month – 10s more than that of a cabin stewardess. At current values, the captain's annual salary of £1,260 would equate to £110,000 or $180,000.

The three senior officers began to operate their daily watches: Chief Officer Wilde, 2–6 each morning and afternoon; First Officer Murdoch, 10–2 each day and night; and Second Officer Lightoller, 6–10 each morning and evening.

The victualling crew of almost 500 was the responsibility of Chief Purser Hugh McElroy (b. 1874, age 37). He had worked for White Star since 1899 and transferred with Smith from *Olympic*. His office was located on C deck, near the forward first-class staircase, next to the enquiry office, from where he and his staff handled a myriad number of passenger requests: rental of rugs and steamer chairs, safekeeping of valuables, currency exchange, dining room table assignments, cabin switches, receipt of letters, cables, telegrams and Marconigrams. Free postcards of the steamer were also always available.

The second-class purser's office was situated on the E deck landing, opposite the second-class staircase, and was under the charge of the assistant purser.

As *Titanic* steamed out into the Atlantic, the passenger lists for first and second classes were issued after dinner and passengers in all three classes settled down to shipboard routine. Very little was organised by the company and, other than impromptu gatherings in third class, there were no dances on board. The ship's orchestra gave concerts in the first and second classes, and the passengers read books or wrote letters, played card games or indulged in more strenuous activities using the ship's facilities or out on the open deck.

Every day, except Sunday, just after 10 a.m., Captain Smith gathered together his chief engineer, purser, assistant purser, surgeon and chief steward and made a departmental inspection of his ship. In the engine

Apart from the smoke from the rear funnel, a remarkably good touched-up photograph of *Titanic*. (Rotary)

THE ILL-FATED WHITE STAR LINER "TITANIC" (45,000 TONS). No. 4
SUNK BY COLLISION WITH AN ICEBERG, APRIL 15th, 1912, WITH A LOSS OF 1,500 SOULS. THE GREATEST
MARITIME DISASTER IN HISTORY.

Titanic at sea. An excellent doctored image, but this is probably *Olympic* on her trials. (Walton)

room only the chief engineer accompanied him. After the thorough inspection, Smith would go over the results with his officers and deal with navigational matters. Whistles were tested every day at 12 noon.

Passengers in third class were awoken at 7.30 a.m., to be followed by another gong thirty minutes later indicating that breakfast was served, after which they went to the open deck promenade areas whilst their stewards tidied the cabins and prepared the dining saloon for lunch. Around 10 a.m. they could return to their quarters and 'dinner' was served at 1 p.m. and 'tea' at 6 p.m. Passengers spent between times either in the two public rooms or back out on the open deck. In the evening they would generally pass away the time providing their own entertainment, lights being turned out at 10.30 p.m. At 11 p.m. the lights were extinguished in the first- and second-class dining saloons, and, with the exception of the first-class smoking room which closed at midnight, all lights in other public rooms were turned off at 11.30 p.m. Bars opened at 8 a.m. and closed at the times detailed above.

Two 'master' clocks were located in the chart room behind the bridge and they were linked to nearly fifty 'slave' clocks throughout the ship. On westbound voyages the ship's official time was changed at midnight, when the clocks were adjusted backwards to reflect the time at noon the following day. On a half-landing of the forward first-class staircase the two sister ships featured a magnificent clock with a wooden statue on either side called 'Honour and Glory crowning Time'. The clock on *Titanic* may not have been ready and was possibly replaced by a mirror. All known photographs that exist are of the clock on *Olympic*.

Deck chairs were hired at a charge of 4s each for the voyage; however, they were not allowed on the boat deck in first class, but on the promenade A deck.

Shuffleboard and deck quoits were popular games on the open boat deck, and the company provided chess sets, draughts and dominoes upon application to the library steward. Card games were popular throughout the classes, but on Sundays games of chance were discouraged in public rooms. At least three professional card players were likely on board and the company had been forced to alert their passengers to this threat by inserting the following into the passenger list:

SPECIAL NOTICE The attention of the managers has been called to the fact that certain persons, believed to be professional gamblers, are in the habit of travelling to and fro in Atlantic steamships. In bringing this to the knowledge of travellers the managers, while not wishing in the slightest degree to interfere with the freedom of action of patrons of the White Star Line, desire to invite their assistance in discouraging games of chance, as being likely to afford these individuals special opportunities for taking unfair advantage of others.

On Saturday 13 April, a fire in the forward coalbunker of boiler room 5 believed to have started in Belfast was at last put out. Internal combustion often occurred on coal-burning ships of the time and the passengers were unaware of the situation.

Olympic superimposed on a rough sea. *Titanic* had calm seas throughout her short life.

R.M.S. TITANIC IN MID-OCEAN

WHITE STAR TRIPLE-SCREW STEAMER "TITANIC" (45,000 TONS).
THE LARGEST VESSEL IN THE WORLD
FIRST VOYAGE FROM SOUTHAMPTON TO NEW YORK, WEDNESDAY, APRIL 10th, 1912.

THIS VESSEL IS LUBRICATED WITH "VACUUM" TURBINE OIL.   VACUUM OIL CO. LTD.
LONDON.

Olympic, again superimposed on a rough sea. This postcard advertises the maiden voyage of *Titanic*. Mr Howard Case (Managing Director of Vacuum Oil Company) was travelling on board and perished. (Wightman, Mountain & Andrews)

In addition to the two doctors on board, the ship was equipped with a small hospital located on D deck starboard just aft of amidships. Medical treatment was chargeable by the company unless the sickness had originated on board, in which case passengers were not charged for treatment or medicine.

Although the elevators were not the first to be installed on passenger liners, they were still innovative and extremely popular; the four lift stewards, William Carney (age 31), Alfred King (18), Reginald Pacey (17) and Frederick Allen (17), were kept busy throughout those days at sea.

All passengers looked forward to receiving the ship's daily newspaper, *The Atlantic Daily Bulletin*, containing, in addition to news items, advertisements and menus from the ship's restaurants.

The ship featured a clothes-pressing and cleaning room:

In the charge of an expert attendant, who will carry out any work of this kind for Ladies and Gentlemen in accordance with a fixed printed tariff of charges which can be found on application to the Bedroom Steward.

Shoes left outside first-class cabins at night were cleaned.

The first-class barber's shop on C-deck port side, and second class on E deck, sold souvenirs of the crossing, many carrying the ship's name as well as the White Star logo.

Unlike ships of today, there was not a laundry service on board either for passengers or the company. All dirty linen was stored on board until the vessel reached port.

The problems with the hot-air heating system had still not been resolved even by Sunday 14 April, which led to complaints from some passengers. This problem was much less noticeable to first-class passengers, their cabins being fitted with self-controlled electric heaters.

The main first-class dining saloon, located on D deck aft of the reception room, had a capacity of over 500 and was one of the two largest dining saloons afloat. Stretching, at single-deck height, from one side of the ship to the other, it was lit by portholes decorated with backlit glass covers. Breakfast was served between 8 and 10 a.m., luncheon at 1 p.m. and dinner at 7 p.m. A bugler playing *Roast Beef of Old England* announced lunch and dinner. Meals in this restaurant were included in the passage cost; however, children were not allowed to eat here unless the full fare had been paid – although this was often overlooked if room was available.

Doubt exists as to the exact colouring of the first-class restaurant on board *Titanic*. The chairs on *Olympic* were in padded green leather that would have clashed with the floor tiles of blue, ochre and red on *Titanic*. A couple of witnesses have stated that the restaurant on *Titanic* was carpeted, unlike the tiled restaurant on *Olympic*, but it is thought that they may have been referring to the B-deck restaurant or the reception room.

The table sizes came in twos, fours, sixes or eights, and Captain Smith favoured a table for six in the forward centre section of the dining room. When required on the bridge or in bad weather, he normally took his meals in his own nearby quarters, provided by his steward.

Passengers in first class dressed formally for dinner except for the first and last nights.

First-class menus have survived for certain days on board *Titanic* and their contents were enormous. Luncheon on Sunday 14 April consisted of two soups, five main choices and three desserts. In addition, there was a buffet offering more than twelve items plus salad and eight different cheeses; the lunch menu also offered 'Iced Draught Munich Lager Beer 3d and 6d a tankard'. Dinner that night was equally impressive but did not offer a buffet or lager beer! Two soups again, following hors d'oeuvres, followed by a choice of seven hot and three cold main courses and four desserts:

> WHITE STAR LINE INFORMATION FOR PASSENGERS: Wines etc. Passengers are requested to sign cards when ordering wines and spirits etc., at table, and accounts for these are presented at the end of the voyage by the table steward or the bedroom steward to whom payment may be made.

The second-class dining saloon, located aft on D deck, was panelled in oak and also extended the width of the ship. With a seating capacity of 394, there would, at times, have been two sittings required. Diners were summoned by gong and would not normally have dressed formally for dinner.

A second-class menu for dinner on the night of 14 April has also survived and features soup, four choices of main course with vegetables and four choices of dessert, followed by nuts, fruit, cheese and coffee. Unlike its first-class counterpart, made of stiff cardboard bordered by a gold edge and carrying the White Star Line and Oceanic Steam Navigation Company (OSNC) logos, the second-class menu for each meal was in the form of a postcard, White Star benefiting from the free advertising.

White Star Line publicity material described the third-class dining room thus:

The third class dining saloon is situated amidships on the middle deck, consisting of two saloons extending from ship's side to ship's side, well lighted with side lights and all finished enamel white; the chairs are of special design. The position of the apartment, in the centre of the ship, illustrates the wonderful strides made in passenger accommodation in modern times. Third class passengers today have greater comfort on the ocean than first class passengers had before the great developments had taken place for which the White Star Line is largely responsible.

The 'room' was, in fact, two rooms separated by a watertight bulkhead. Located on F deck amidships, the dining rooms were fitted with separate chairs rather than the benches of earlier vessels. In common with company practice, single men would use one room, with women and families in the other. All passengers were seated at long tables each accommodating twenty and, with a seating capacity of 473, two sittings would have been required. Indeed, had the ship been full, three sittings would have been necessary.

Third-class diners on *Titanic* would probably have followed these times for their meals: breakfast, 8–10 a.m.; lunch, 1–2.30 p.m.; and dinner, 6–7.30 p.m. Their menu, however, would reflect breakfast, dinner, tea and supper in that order, and would also have been a postcard but featuring all of the day's meals on one card. The third-class menu for 14 April lists:

BREAKFAST
Oatmeal Porridge & Milk, Smoked Herrings, Jacket Potatoes, Ham & Eggs, Fresh Bread & Butter, Marmalade, Swedish Bread, Tea & Coffee.

DINNER
Rice Soup, Fresh Bread, Cabin Biscuits, Roast Beef, Brown Gravy, Sweet Corn, Boiled Potatoes, Plum Pudding, Sweet Sauces and Fruit.

TEA
Cold Meat, Cheese, Pickles, Fresh Bread & Butter, Stewed Figs and Rice, Tea.

SUPPER
Gruel, Cabin Biscuits and Cheese

Each menu carries the wording, 'Any complaint respecting the food supplied, want of attention or incivility, should be at once reported to the Purser or Chief Steward. For purposes of identification, each steward wears a numbered badge on the arm.'

The last of the four passenger restaurants is often referred to as the à la carte restaurant, but the White Star Line in 1912 used the term 'First Class Restaurant'. This B-deck restaurant had windows, unlike the 'hidden' portholes of the first-class dining saloon. With walnut panelling and Dubarry Rose carpeting, the popular restaurant seated up to 137 people at forty-nine tables. Open daily for first-class passengers from 8 a.m. to 11 p.m., meals were obtained at set prices. Reservations, made through the manager M. Luigi Gatti, were usually required. If, at time of booking, passengers indicated that they would be using this facility throughout the voyage, they were offered a discount on their passage tickets. Both this restaurant, and the adjacent Café

Parisien, were popular with the younger wealthy passengers on board; they offered food from the same menu and were operated as a concession by M. Gatti and his sixty-six-strong staff of predominantly Italian or French nationals. It is thought that the waiters received a wage of 1s per voyage but were well compensated with tips. Different menus and crockery from that of the White Star Line identified the restaurant.

M. Gatti had come from a well-known London restaurant, Oddenino's Imperial, located at 60–62 Regent Street, London.

The first company and vessel to offer this à la carte facility had been *Amerika* of the Hamburg America Line in 1905. The restaurant there was run by Ritz-Carlton and that is probably why the similar restaurants on *Olympic* and *Titanic* are sometimes incorrectly referred to as the Ritz restaurants.

Aft of the smoking room, on A deck was the Verandah Café, also known as the Palm Court. Furnished with trellises and climbing plants, light refreshments, but not large meals, could be purchased here between the hours of 8 a.m. and 11 p.m. Located either side of the second-class entrance, this first-class facility could, on good days, be opened to the air. Smoking was not allowed on the starboard side and access to both sides was through draught-proof revolving doors.

Much of the vast amount of food carried was stored in the ship's refrigerated provision stores on G deck. Examples of this include 40,000 eggs, 1,500 gallons of milk, 75,000lb of meat, 25,000lb of poultry and game, 36,000 oranges and 7,000 heads of lettuce. Additionally, the ship carried 850 bottles of spirits, 20,000 bottles of beer, 1,500 bottles of wine and 15,000 bottles of mineral water.

Two groups, of five and three musicians, provided music in the first and second class. All eight were employed by an agency in Liverpool and, travelling as second-class passengers, they each received £4 per month. The quintet, led by bandmaster and lead violinist Wallace Hartley (age 33), comprised two violinists, one cellist, one double bass player and one pianist, and the trio consisted of one violinist, one cellist and one pianist. Four Steinway pianos were located throughout the ship, in the first-class entrance hall reception room and in the B-deck restaurant and dining saloon, the latter being used only for Divine Service. The other two were located in the second-class dining saloon and entrance hall, and in the third-class general room.

In addition to Wallace Hartley, the band included William Brailey (piano), Roger Bricoux (cello), John Clarke (bass), John Hume (violin), George Kriss (violin), Percy Taylor (cello) and John Woodward (cello). Some were able to play on more than one instrument.

Neither of the two groups played in the first-class dining saloon, but the trio played in the reception area of the B-deck restaurant. The two groups each played for just over six hours a day. The quintet played from 10 to 11 a.m. in the aft second-class entrance foyer on C deck and then moved to the first-class entrance hall on the boat deck. From 4 to 5 p.m. they played in the first-class reception room before returning to the aft second-class entrance from 5 to 6 p.m. From 8 p.m. to 9.15 p.m. they gave a concert in the first-class reception room before finishing off for an hour again in second class. It was usual on any crossing for a collection to be taken up for the ship's orchestra.

By noon on Friday 12 April, the first day's run was posted at 484 miles, travelling at an average speed of just under 21 knots. With a clear sky and temperature rising to 60°F, clouds had built up that afternoon as the ship headed into a 20-knot wind. At noon on Saturday 13 April, *Titanic* had made 519 miles at a similar speed. Her engine output was now increased from 72 to 75rpm. After the cloud broke up at dawn, the temperature rose again to approximately 60°F at noon, but the sky became cloudy that night.

At noon on Sunday 14 April *Titanic* had posted 546 miles at an average speed of 22.5 knots. It became clear that, unless she reduced her speed, she would arrive in New York late on Tuesday night, 16 April, instead of her scheduled arrival the following morning:

WHITE STAR LINE NOTICE: LANDING ARRANGEMENTS AT NEW YORK

Should the steamer arrive at the New York wharf after 8.00pm, passengers may land if they wish to do so, and have their baggage passed the following morning not earlier than 7 o'clock. Breakfast will be served to those who remain on board overnight.

Evidence points to Ismay's hope that *Titanic* would beat her sister and arrive in New York on Tuesday evening.

Sunday 14 April dawned sunny and bright with a calm sea and it became clear to passengers that the speed was increasing and there were rumours suggesting a 'speed run' the following day. On that Sunday the final three of the ship's double-ended boilers had been lit, bringing the total to twenty-four. Possibly the following day, the remaining five single-ended auxiliary boilers would also be brought into use.

Captain Smith conducted Divine Service at 10.30 a.m. in the first-class dining saloon, ending at 11.15 a.m., and members of the ship's orchestra were in attendance to accompany the hymns. Assistant Purser Reginald Barker conducted an Episcopalian service in second class and Father Thomas Byles led a Catholic Mass in the second-class lounge, later moving to third class to conduct another Mass.

After lunch, passengers began to notice a definite chill in the air and sought the warmth of the ship's interiors. By 7.30 p.m. the air temperature was 33°F.

That evening, in the B-deck restaurant, a group of wealthy American passengers had organised a meal together to which they had invited Captain Smith. It has been suggested that the meal was in Smith's honour but there is little evidence to support this.

Designer Thomas Andrews and the ship's surgeon, Dr O'Loughlin, had dined together, after which Andrews returned to his cabin to continue with his work, ironing out any glitches that came up during the maiden voyage.

In second class, Reverend Ernest Carter organised hymn singing, attended by at least 100 passengers. The singing had gone on a bit longer than intended and, after 10 p.m., refreshments were served.

The third-class general room had been the venue for a great amount of singing and dancing that evening but, as ten o'clock drew near, the ship began to quieten down.

By 11.30 that night the passengers who were still up and about were being reminded by the stewards that the lights would shortly be extinguished. The water temperature had fallen to 28°F and the sea had become an icy black calm.

Titanic was steaming at over 22 knots: faster than she had ever travelled before.

five

WARNINGS

White Star Line passenger vessels in 1912 carried Marconi wireless communication facilities. On board *Titanic*, the wireless office was located on the boat deck about 40ft behind the bridge and, as there was no telephone link between the two, any messages to or from the bridge were taken by hand. The wireless cabin consisted of three rooms, one for the equipment, one operating room and one sleeping cabin shared by the two operators, employed by Marconi and travelling as second-class passengers.

In 1909, Jack Binns, the Marconi operator on board the White Star vessel *Baltic*, was credited with the saving of several thousand lives after the collision between the White Star liner *Republic* and the Italian emigrant ship *Florida*.

On *Titanic*, John (Jack) Phillips (age 25) was the senior man earning £4 5s per month, assisted by his deputy Harold Bride (22) earning £2 2s 6d per month. The range of their equipment was estimated to be about 400 miles by day and up to 1,000 miles at night, due to there being much less wireless traffic overnight.

BALTIC

Built in 1904 at Harland and Wolff, Belfast, the 23,876grt *Baltic* was the third vessel of what became known as the 'Big Four', built for the White Star Line, who, wanting her to be the largest ship in the world, asked her builders to lengthen her by 28ft during her construction. This lengthening resulted in a slower speed, requiring her main engines to be modified.

A twin-screw vessel, carrying over 2,700 passengers and 560 crew, with eight holds, she had an enormous cargo capacity.

In January 1909 she assisted in the rescue of survivors after the collision between White Star's *Republic* and Lloyd Italiano's *Florida*.

After acting as a troopship during the First World War, she resumed her transatlantic schedule until being laid up in September 1932.

In February 1933 she departed Liverpool for scrapping in Osaka, Japan.

Apart from ship–shore communications, the main purpose of the Marconi Company was to earn money from the ship's passengers. Handwritten messages were handed in at the enquiry office, charges calculated at 12*s* 6*d* for the first ten words and 9*d* for each subsequent word and the message was sent to the Marconi office for transmission. Incoming messages for passengers were typed on to a Marconi form and sent to the enquiry office, from where it would be sent to the addressee. Navigational messages were taken to the bridge along a corridor on the port side of the officers' quarters.

The following extract is taken from a pilot book printed, in 1909, by the Hydrographic Office of the British Admiralty:

> One of the chief dangers in crossing the Atlantic lies in the probability of encountering masses of ice, both in the form of bergs and of extensive fields of solid compact ice, released at the breaking up of winter in Arctic regions and drifted down by the Labrador Current across their direct route between April and August, both months inclusive.

Marconi himself had intended to travel on the maiden voyage of *Titanic* but, after the date change from March to April, chose Cunard's *Lusitania* instead.

Late at night on Saturday 13 April, the wireless transmitter failed. For almost seven hours Phillips and Bride worked hard at tracing and repairing the fault, which turned out to be short-circuiting in one of the secondary circuits. By the time the fault was repaired a considerable backlog of messages had built up.

At about 10.30 p.m., the Furness Withy vessel *Rappahannock*, eastbound to Europe from Halifax, passed the westbound *Titanic* and sent her the following message by Morse lamp: 'Have just passed through heavy field ice and several icebergs.' *Titanic* replied: 'Message received. Thank you. Good night.' There is doubt as to the veracity of this message, but it does seem that the *Rappahannock* was probably the last vessel to have seen *Titanic*. Furness Withy stated that none of their vessels were involved in the disaster.

The Furness Withy eastbound steamer *Rappahannock* passed *Titanic* during the night of Saturday 13 April. (Peabody Essex Museum, Salem, MA)

On the previous day, 12 April, *Titanic* had received the first wireless message indicating that ice lay ahead. Captain Caussin of the French liner *La Touraine* (call sign MLT) had sent the following to *Titanic* (MGY), received at 5.46 p.m.: 'Crossed thick ice field Lat. 44.58 Long. 50.40. Saw another ice field and two icebergs Lat. 45.20 Long. 45.09.'

Titanic replied at 6.21 p.m.: 'Thanks for your message and information. Had fine weather. (Smith).' Both these messages carried the prefix MSG, meaning 'Captain to Captain', thus requiring the wireless operator to deliver the message to the captain.

The first wireless ice warning on Sunday 14 April was with the MSG signal from Captain Barr of the Cunard liner *Caronia* (MRA) at 9.12 a.m.: 'Westbound steamers report bergs, growlers and field ice in 42 N from 49 to 51 W.'

France's *La Touraine* radioed an ice warning to *Titanic* at 5.46 p.m. on Friday 12 April. (L&L)

115. **Le Havre.** — « La Touraine », Compagnie Générale Transatlantique. — L. et L. Havre, déposé

Cunard Line's *Caronia* was the first to send an ice warning by radio on Sunday 14 April and also heard the first distress calls.

Holland America Line's *Noordam* sent the second ice warning to *Titanic* via *Caronia* at 11.47 a.m. on Sunday 14 April.

Titanic replied at 10.28 a.m.: 'Thanks for message and information. Have had variable weather throughout. (Smith).' Captain Smith showed this message to Lightoller, who later stated that this was the first that he knew of ice ahead.

At 11.47 a.m. *Titanic* time, another MSG signal was received, this time from Captain Krol of the Dutch liner *Noordam* (MHA) via Cunard's *Caronia*: 'Congratulations on new command. Much ice reported in Lat. 42.24 to 42.45 N and Long. 49.50 to 50.20 W.'

Titanic replied at 12.31 p.m., also via *Caronia*: 'Many thanks. Had moderate variable weather throughout. (Smith).'

The third warning received that Sunday came from the German liner *Amerika* (DDR) at 1.49 p.m., asking that *Titanic* forward the message to the Hydrographic Office in Washington DC via Cape Race: 'Amerika passed two large icebergs in 41.27N, 50.8W on the 14th April.' Captain Knuth had addressed his message MSG but there is no further evidence as to what happened to it except that the wireless operator on *Titanic* did forward the transmission. Important messages should be displayed on the bridge for all to see.

One of the more controversial ice warnings came from White Star Line's *Baltic* (MBC), received at 1.54 p.m. and addressed MSG from her captain, Ronson: 'Greek steamer "Athenai" (MTI) reports passing icebergs and large quantities of field ice today in Lat. 41.51N. Long. 49.52W. Wish you and Titanic all success.' This indicated that *Titanic* was heading straight for the ice.

Germany's *Amerika* asked *Titanic* to forward to the Hydrographic Office in Washington DC the information that she had passed two large icebergs, giving their position. *Amerika*, when built in 1905–06, at 22,225grt, was the largest vessel in the world. She had a varied career, having been taken over by the USA in 1917 and operated by them as *America*. She was broken up in 1957.

9113. S.S "Amerika" at Prince of Wales Pier. Dover.

The message was taken directly to Captain Smith who, shortly after receiving the Marconigram, handed it to Bruce Ismay, who silently read it and put it in his pocket. We shall never know why Smith allowed Ismay to keep the message for so long; he eventually asked for its return around 7.15 that evening, nor is there evidence that the message was finally posted on the bridge.

Titanic did reply at 2.57 p.m.: 'Thanks for your message and good wishes. Had fine weather since leaving. (Smith).'

First-class passenger Mrs Emily Ryerson stated, at the Limitation of Liability Hearings, that Ismay had told her and Mrs Marion Thayer, 'We are in among the icebergs. We are not going very fast, 20 or 21 knots, but we are going to start up some extra boilers this evening.' He took the Marconigram from his pocket and showed it to the two ladies.

The important fifth message received that day by *Titanic* was, in fact, intercepted at 7.37 p.m., as it had been sent MSG from Captain Lord on the Leyland liner *Californian* (MWL) to Captain Japha of Leyland's *Antillian* (MJL), eastbound from New Orleans to Liverpool: 'Three large icebergs five miles to southward of us. Lat. 42.3N Long. 49.9W.' The three icebergs would thus be at 41.48 N 49.09 W.

10. – S. S. Baltic at Landing stage, Liverpool

Copyright G. Cook

The ice warning from *Baltic* (1904), third and slowest of White Star's 'Big Four', stayed in Bruce Ismay's pocket for most of Sunday 14 April. (J.D. Grant)

Antillian replied half an hour later to Lord: 'Thanks for the info. Seen no ice. Bon voyage. Japha.'

Second Marconi operator Bride does remember taking the intercepted message to the bridge but was unable to say to whom it was given. At 9.32 p.m. *Titanic* forwarded *Amerika*'s ice report on to the Hydrographic Office in Washington DC via Cape Race.

At 9.52 p.m. the sixth ice warning was received, from Atlantic Transport Line's steamer *Mesaba* (MMV). The message did not carry the prefix MSG, nor was it taken to the bridge. It read: 'In Lat. 42N to 41.25N. Long. 49W to 50.30 W. Saw much heavy pack ice and great number of large icebergs, also field ice. Weather good, clear.' The message was addressed specifically to *Titanic*. Bride, working alone as Phillips slept after their long night of wireless repairs, acknowledged receipt of this message and continued to work on the backlog of outgoing messages.

Lightoller is believed to have written later: 'It was Phillips' failure to pass on the *Mesaba*'s warning that doomed the *Titanic*: The position given was right ahead of us and not many miles distant.' It should be pointed out here, however, that the Marconi wireless operators had received no navigational training and the latitude and longitude figures, in wireless messages received, would not have conveyed to them the presence of danger.

Probably the most important ice warning was sent by Atlantic Transport's *Mesaba* and was received by *Titanic* less than two hours before the collision. The message was not addressed to the captain and remained in the Marconi room. (W. Haynes)

R.M.S. Mesaba

MESABA

The 6,833grt *Mesaba* was built in 1898 by Harland and Wolff, Belfast, for the Wilson & Furness-Leyland Line and was acquired by the Atlantic Transport Line. This 13-knot vessel was primarily designed to carry cargo but did have accommodation for saloon passengers in thirty-seven cabins. The ice-warning message to *Titanic* was sent by her wireless operator Stanley Adams at 7.50 p.m. on the night of 14 April 1912 and received at 9.40 p.m., two hours before the collision with the iceberg.

In September 1918, whilst in convoy from Liverpool to Philadelphia, she was torpedoed and sunk by the German submarine *UB118* in St George's Channel. Twenty people died in the loss of *Mesaba*, including her captain.

Finally, a casual Cyril Evans on board *Californian* sent a message to *Titanic* at 11.07 p.m., with no MSG prefix or advised position: 'Say, old man, we are stopped and surrounded by ice.' The response to this loud message – *Californian* was not very far away – was: 'Shut up, shut up, I am busy; I am working Cape Race.'

Despite the ice warnings received from vessels ahead, few seem to have appreciated their importance. Replies, when they were given, had an air of casualness about them. Smith did continue on his southerly course for longer than usual and waited for possibly an additional forty-five minutes before turning west towards New York at 5.50 p.m. It is thought that this delay in turning was to try to avoid the ice field ahead. But with only three men, two in the crow's nest and one on the bridge, keeping a lookout in clear, calm weather, it was decided to maintain course and speed.

As evening fell, all aboard saw a magnificent sunset, by which time the breeze that had been blowing all day began to lessen and the temperature continued to fall. The last three main boilers had been fired up and the speed continued to increase. Murdoch asked that the fore-scuttle hatch be closed as the glow would make seeing forward in the dark more difficult: 'We are in the vicinity of ice and I want everything dark before the bridge.' When Boxhall relieved Pitman on duty at 8 p.m. the temperature had fallen to 31.5°F and the ship was forging ahead at 21.5 knots.

Smith came on to the bridge at about 9 p.m. and discussed the weather conditions with Lightoller, who felt that the calm sea would mean that there would be no waves breaking against the base of a berg, making it more difficult to detect. Less than half an hour later Smith left the bridge, leaving Lightoller with these words: 'If it becomes at all doubtful let me know at once; I will be just inside.' Lightoller then asked Moody to call the men in the crow's nest and tell them to keep a sharp lookout for ice, particularly small ice and growlers (or icebergs).

Murdoch relieved Lightoller at 10 p.m. and together they discussed how difficult it was to see the horizon, and the calmness of the water, making it harder to see any icebergs. Captain Smith did not feel it necessary to slow his ship down under the circumstances, but assumed that his officers and the lookouts would be able to see any dangers ahead in time to avoid them. As Murdoch replaced Lightoller, so lookouts Frederick Fleet and Reginald Lee replaced Archie Jewell and George Symons, and Quartermaster Hichens relieved Quartermaster Olliver at the wheel.

In the Marconi room, Phillips, now on duty, continued to send private messages on to the station at Cape Race for forwarding. Marconi operator Cyril Evans, on board the stationary *Californian* nearby, heard some of these messages, turned off his set and went to bed.

It was just after 11.30 p.m. and most of the passengers and crew on *Titanic* had also gone to bed.

six

COLLISION

Three times the brass bell in the crow's nest rang. Frederick Fleet, in the biting wind, had seen a large black mass loom up directly in the path of *Titanic*. He had rung the bell three times immediately to warn the bridge. Once would have indicated something to port and twice to starboard. Almost at the same time he telephoned the bridge and reported to Moody 'Iceberg right ahead'. On such a night, the average iceberg would be visible from about half a nautical mile, and when the bell rang the iceberg was about a third of a nautical mile (2,000ft) ahead of the ship. The bridge was almost 65ft from the waterline and the lookouts were about 20ft higher. Moody passed on the information to Murdoch, who had almost certainly seen the iceberg himself by this time.

Murdoch's first action was to order the helmsman Hichens 'Hard a Starboard'. Hichens would have turned the wheel to port, which then would have turned the vessel to port, the helm (or tiller) having gone to starboard. Sixth Officer Moody was standing right next to Hichens and any incorrect turns on the quartermaster's part would have been instantly identified. There is no evidence to indicate that 'the wheel was turned the wrong way'. Nearly thirty seconds had elapsed between the bell warning and the helm being put hard over. As the wheelhouse, behind the bridge, was enclosed, Hichens would not have been able to see what lay ahead but just had to obey the wheel orders from the officer on watch.

At the same time as ordering the helmsman to turn, Murdoch swung the engine room telegraph to 'Stop'. The only person to testify that further orders 'Full Astern' were made was Boxhall, not one of the surviving boiler room or engine room staff stating that they received the order to go full astern before the impact.

Murdoch's intention was to 'port round' the iceberg and, at the moment of impact, he had already ordered Hichens to swing 'Hard a Port' with the intention of swinging the stern away from the iceberg. Had he ordered 'Full Astern', he would have had to stop all three propellers from turning before the two outer propellers began to turn in reverse. An unlikely situation!

Lookout Lee, in the crow's nest, is quoted as saying: 'It was a dark mass that came through that haze and there was no white appearing until it was just close alongside the ship.'

Quartermaster Rowe, on the aft docking bridge, saw the iceberg pass by on the starboard side and thought it to be almost 100ft high. Other reports suggest that the berg was slightly higher than the boat deck or the bridge.

Down below, the boiler room staff heard the bells ringing, giving them notice that the watertight doors were about to close. On the bridge the switch was pulled that released the watertight-compartment doors.

An artist's impression, at the time, of the damage caused by the collision with the iceberg. (*Scientific American*)

In all probability a massive, projecting, underwater shelf of the iceberg with which she collided tore open several compartments of the "Titanic," the rent extending from near the bow to amidships. The energy of the blow, 1,161,000 foot-tons, was equal to that of the combined broadsides of the "Delaware" and "North Dakota."

Since the sighting of the iceberg, the bow had begun to swing to port and the iceberg impacted along the starboard side. It was approximately 11.40 p.m. and the ship's speed had dropped to about 20.5 knots.

Actual contact with the iceberg lasted about seven seconds but damage occurred to the Forepeak Tank, No. 1 Hold, No. 2 Hold, No. 3 Hold, No. 6 Boiler Room and the forward starboard bunker in No. 5 Boiler Room. At each impact, the ship's rivets snapped and seams split, causing seawater to enter the vessel. It is thought that only 12sq. ft of damage was caused over a distance of some 200ft. As the iceberg passed by, a considerable amount of ice fell off on to the forecastle head and the forward well deck.

Titanic was designed to float with any three of her first five compartments open to the sea, but with this damage she was doomed. It has been suggested that the rudder size was insufficient to prevent disaster but this is not so as, even today, a rudder of that size would have passed scrutiny.

Within seconds, a fully clothed Smith appeared on the bridge asking what had happened. Murdoch gave him the news of the sighting, his attempts to avoid the iceberg, the impact and that he had closed the watertight doors.

As the iceberg disappeared into the darkness astern, the vessel almost immediately developed a five-degree list to starboard.

The lower a person was in the vessel, the more obvious the extent of damage. Very few of the passengers were aware of the danger but down below, within ten minutes of the impact, there were areas in the forward part of the ship that were already 6ft deep in water. The ship's pumps were started almost immediately but they were only able to handle approximately 4 per cent of the water pouring in. It is thought that the flooding of the ship was at a rate of just over 11 tons of water per second.

Among the first to become aware of the seriousness of the situation were the five postal workers, three American and two British. The mail hold, just below their sorting office on G deck, was located on the orlop deck and it was already beginning to flood. The five men struggled to haul bags out of the advancing water but it was already rising into G deck.

The ship came to a halt facing north-north-west. Steam pressure began to build and the automatic safety valves on each boiler sent the excess steam up to the outlets on the funnels, making such a noise that conversation became very difficult.

The third-class passengers, accommodated in the forward and aft sections of the lowest decks, felt the collision almost as it happened, whereas in second class the stopping of the engines seemed to cause more consternation. In first class, however, it appears that only those still awake – the card players in the smoking room – were aware of the incident but, after discovering what had caused the 'upset', many returned to their card games despite some having seen the iceberg disappear astern. Off-duty officers either noticed or were awakened by a 'jar' or 'slight vibration'.

Most of the first-class passengers were in bed at the time of the collision but were awoken by a shudder or a shake rather than undue noise, unless it was the silence that followed the cessation of the engines. Many, upon asking, were told that there was nothing serious to report and even to go back to bed.

Whereas the majority of the watertight doors had been closed automatically from the bridge, there were ten doors on F deck and nine on E deck that required closing individually by hand. Witnesses later described seeing men struggling to close them; however, the two or three main staircases on board meant that the vessel contained several open areas.

Second-class passenger Lawrence Beesley, in his book *The Loss of the SS Titanic*, described the scene thus:

> A ship that had come quietly to rest without any indication of disaster – no iceberg visible, no hole in the ship's side through which water was pouring in, nothing broken or out of place, no sound of alarm, no panic, no movement of anyone except at a walking pace.

Initially Smith had restarted the engines by signalling 'Slow Ahead' to the engine room. Shortly afterwards the engine room acknowledged 'Stop', after which the ship's engines never operated again.

Bruce Ismay, with an overcoat over his pyjamas, left his suite for the bridge in order to discover what had occurred. He arrived on the bridge to be told by Smith that *Titanic* had struck ice and the situation was believed to be serious, whereupon Ismay returned to his suite. However, on his way back, he met Chief Engineer Joseph Bell and asked him if the ship was badly damaged. Bell told him that he hoped that the ship's pumps could deal with the water.

Most passengers had no idea of the seriousness of the situation and many steerage men had already appeared on the forward well deck to play with the ice.

Boxhall, who had been in the chartroom aft of the bridge at the time of impact, went below to inspect the damage. He got as far as F deck without detecting any damage and was about to return to the bridge when he met Postal Clerk John Smith, who told him that the mail room was flooding. Upon investigation, Boxhall heard the water entering the orlop deck, saw the mail bags floating about and noticed that the water was about to enter G deck. By five minutes to midnight the first-class baggage room on G deck began to flood.

Smith and Thomas Andrews together went below to assess the damage for themselves. Water was visibly coming into the first five compartments at an uncontrollable rate. The weight of this water would pull the vessel down until it spilled over into the next compartment and so on until the she foundered. With both men aware that *Titanic* carried sufficient lifeboats for only half of those on board, Andrews informed Smith that he calculated that the ship would stay afloat for another ninety minutes at most. Few believed at the time that *Titanic* was sinking. Boxhall, on asking Smith if the situation was serious, was told, 'Mr Andrews tells me he gives her from an hour to an hour and a half.'

seven

SO NEAR AND YET SO FAR

In the Marconi room the two operators had finally repaired the wireless equipment early on Sunday morning, 14 April. Throughout that Sunday the two men worked hard to reduce the backlog. Bride, aware of Phillips' tiredness, had offered to replace his senior partner on duty at midnight instead of the scheduled 2 a.m., so went to bed that night around 9 p.m.

On his way back to the bridge, Smith called in at the Marconi room to tell the operators that *Titanic* had struck an iceberg and they should prepare to send out the necessary signal for distress. Smith returned at around 12.10 a.m. and, mentioning that the ship had been seriously damaged, told the operators to send out the first of the distress signals.

North German Lloyd's *Frankfurt*: one of the first vessels to hear the distress call from *Titanic*. (Shearan)

France's *La Provence* heard the CQD while en route from New York to Le Havre. (LL)

There were as many as thirty vessels in the North Atlantic that night, not all of which had a twenty-four-hour radio watch as larger ships such as *Titanic* did.

The first call for assistance was logged at 12.27 a.m. and contained Smith's initial position calculation of 41.44 N, 50.24 W, preceded by the code CQD (CQ – All Stations, D – Distress), and the ship's call sign MGY. Meanwhile, Boxhall had recalculated their position as 41.46 N, 50.14 W, and within ten minutes this would be the accepted position for the remainder of the night. We now know, since the location of the wreck was discovered in 1985, that the first location was 20 nautical miles west of the wreck and the second, Boxhall's, was 13 nautical miles west.

The Marconi International Marine Co. had been using the CQD distress call since 1904 but the German government, preventing the Marconi Company from dominating the ocean's steamers, proposed an alternative at the 1906 Berlin International Wireless Telegraph Convention. Thus was born the famous SOS signal. Britain had accepted this change as far back as 1908 but, even in 1912, the Marconi operators had been slow to put this amendment into practice. This was not the first time that the code SOS was used at sea, but the Marconi operators on *Titanic* did use both CQD and later SOS during the night.

After the first distress call was sent out at 12.27 a.m. ship's time, the alarming news was received not only by ships at sea but also by the radio station at Cape Race, Newfoundland. Amongst the first vessels to receive the call was the German *Frankfurt* (DFT), eastbound from Galveston to Bremerhaven. She was 140 miles to the south-west of the first position location. The French Line's *La Provence* (MLP), also eastbound, from New York to Le Havre, was 60 miles away upon receipt of the CQD.

The third vessel to receive that first CQD was Canadian Pacific's *Mount Temple* (MLQ). The 8,790-ton emigrant ship had departed Antwerp on 3 April for St John, New Brunswick, continuing on to Halifax carrying almost 1,500 predominantly third-class passengers and a crew of approximately 150. Equipped with twenty lifeboats, she had a single yellow funnel and four masts.

Another German vessel, the eastbound *Ypiranga* (DYA), received the first CQD message and, eight minutes later, the second with the amended co-ordinates.

Cunard's *Caronia* (MRA), eastbound for Liverpool from New York, had been one of the vessels to forward ice warnings to *Titanic* and was over 700 miles to the east when she received the distress call.

Asian (MKL) received the CQD message at 12.30 a.m. *Titanic* time. She was westbound, towing the crippled German tanker *Deutschland* to Halifax, and approximately 325 miles south-west of the given position.

Ten minutes after the initial distress call, Cunard's *Carpathia* (MPA), eastbound for Mediterranean ports from New York, received the call giving Boxhall's amended location. She was 58 miles away.

Caronia forwarded the CQD to one of Smith's earlier commands, the White Star liner *Baltic* (MBC), eastbound from New York to Liverpool. Upon receipt *Baltic* attempted to contact *Titanic* at around 1 a.m. She was almost 250 miles away.

At the same time, 12.37 a.m, the Russian–American liner *Birma* (SBA), eastbound from New York to Rotterdam and Libau, received the distress call. She was 107 miles south-west of the amended location.

Olympic (MKC), eastbound from New York to Southampton, was over 500 miles away when she first received news of the collision.

Another White Star vessel, *Celtic* (MLC), a near sister of *Baltic*, was just under 800 miles away, westbound to New York from Liverpool, to the east of *Titanic* when she heard the news.

Below left: Canadian Pacific's *Mount Temple*, carrying 1,500 immigrants to Canada, was amongst the first to hear the distress call. (Hy Richards)

Below right: Hapag's *Ypiranga*, another German vessel, received both distress positions from *Titanic*.

Ten minutes later, at 1.07 a.m., the German *Cincinnati* (DDC) was over 300 miles south-west of the location when she received the CQD call.

Of these vessels, five – *La Provence*, *Caronia*, *Asian* (towing), *Celtic* and *Cincinnati* – took no further action as they considered that they were too far away, other ships were nearer and thus were more able to render assistance.

The Allan liner *Virginian*, eastbound for Liverpool from St John and Halifax, was 178 miles away when she received the CQD at 1.12 a.m. *Titanic* time. Two minutes later she tried to reply but was unable to reach the stricken ship, so contacted the radio station at Cape Race and asked that they inform *Titanic* that she was 170 miles to the north and was coming to her aid. When only 25 miles away, at 11 a.m. on 15 April, she was told by *Carpathia* to return to her original course. *Virginian* last heard from *Titanic* at 2.12 a.m.

Throughout the next two hours there would be almost seventy distress calls:

We require assistance, I require assistance immediately, Come at once, We have struck a berg, It's a CQD old man, Require immediate assistance, We have collision with iceberg, sinking, Captain says get your boats ready, Going down at the head, What is your position? We are putting the women off in small boats, Flooded, Women and children in boats cannot last much longer MGY, Engine room full up to the boilers.

Initially the noise of escaping steam made it very difficult to hear the replies to the distress calls.

Frankfurt, the German vessel that received the first distress message, had originally sent a message of greeting before receiving the CQD. Phillips replied asking for her location, not knowing that, at the time, *Frankfurt* was unaware of the situation. Eventually *Frankfurt* replied that she had altered course and was making for *Titanic*, but she arrived too late to be of any help. One last message from the *Frankfurt* was received towards the end. It seems that *Frankfurt*, not hearing some of the later messages due to the stricken

Above left: Leyland Line's *Asian* was towing the crippled German tanker *Deutschland* when she received the news.

Above: Cunard's *Carpathia* was 58 miles away, en route to the Mediterranean from New York, when she received the second location message. (Stepancick)

77

Virginian, having received the distress call, was unable to contact *Titanic* so tried through the radio station at Cape Race. (Kingsway)

MOUNT TEMPLE

SS *Mount Temple* was built by Armstrong-Whitworth in 1901 for the Beaver Line and purchased by Canadian Pacific in 1903. The 8,790grt twin-screw vessel had a top speed of 13 knots and was designed to carry approximately 1,260 passengers, mostly emigrants in third class.

In 1907 the vessel ran aground off Nova Scotia and, although no lives were lost in the accident, she was not refloated until 1908.

At the outbreak of the First World War she was fitted with a 3in gun on her stern, primarily for defence use. In December 1916, whilst eastbound with a cargo of horses in the mid-Atlantic, she was targetted by a German surface raider, which scuttled the vessel and her cargo with explosives. Over a hundred people were taken off prior to her scuttling and, other than the US citizens who were released, most were interned for the duration of the war.

liner's failing power system, sent the friendly 'What's up old man?' only to receive Phillips' frustrated reply, 'You fool, stand by and keep out.'

Captain Moore on *Mount Temple* turned his ship and made for the amended location to the south-west nearly 50 miles away. He raised his officers and crew, prepared the gangway for lowering, had all possible lifeboats uncovered and swung out, and rigged ropes and ladders over the side. Sadly, at about 4.45 a.m., his ship was blocked by an enormous expanse of pack ice and was unable to take any further part in the proceedings. She last heard from *Titanic* at 1.49 a.m.

Ypiranga altered course and made for the location but was still over 50 miles away when the awful truth became known. She last heard from *Titanic* at 1.52 a.m.

After attempting to make contact at around 1 a.m., *Baltic* turned and made for the CQD location. By 9.15 a.m., and after steaming for 134 miles, she resumed her original journey after *Carpathia* informed her that she was not required.

Birma also altered course and made for *Titanic* in a journey that would take her over seven hours and have her arriving on the scene too late to be of any help. She last heard from the liner at 1.55 a.m.

On board *Olympic*, 500 miles away, an incredulous Captain Haddock ordered all boilers lit and sped his ship to the scene. By Monday afternoon he had heard from *Carpathia* that *Titanic* had sunk and that all surviving passengers and crew had been picked up. The powerful radio apparatus on *Olympic* had last received a message from her sister ship at 1.57 a.m.

Leyland Line's SS *Californian*, commanded by Captain Stanley Lord, had left London on 5 April and was making for Boston. She had accommodation for forty-seven passengers, but on this voyage was carrying none. This four-masted vessel, with a single pink funnel, came to a stop against an enormous field of pack ice blocking her route at 10.20 p.m. on that Sunday night and Lord wisely decided to wait until daylight before trying to negotiate the ice field.

Once *Titanic* had come to a final stop, the lookouts in her crow's nest indicated, by ringing their bell once, that they could see an object off the port bow. Boxhall, having now returned to the bridge, claimed that he could see the vessel with the naked eye but, with the use of binoculars, could make out two masthead lights.

Third Officer Groves on *Californian*, which had a lifeboat capacity of 218, pointed out to Lord an approaching 'passenger steamer coming up on us' on their starboard beam. Later, at approximately 11.52 p.m. (11.40 p.m. *Titanic* time), Groves saw that the steamer had stopped and her deck lights seemed to be out. *Titanic* had a list of 5 degrees.

Initially Boxhall was ordered to try to contact her by Morse lamp with the message, 'Come at once, we are sinking'. He, and also some passengers, thought that there was a Morse reply but the message was indiscernible.

At around 12.45 a.m. on the aft docking bridge, Quartermaster George Rowe telephoned the bridge to say that he had seen a lifeboat in the water. Boxhall asked him to come to the bridge and, if he knew where they were kept, to bring distress rockets. Armed with a box of twelve socket signals, Rowe made his way forward and, for the next hour, he, Boxhall and Quartermaster Bright tried to contact the 'mystery vessel' with rockets in addition to Morse signalling.

The passengers, now assembling on the boat deck, would have seen the lights off the port bow offering a semblance of hope, but the rockets would also have clearly indicated that their ship was in danger.

The first of eight rockets took off from a railing on the bridge at about 12.47 a.m. Having reached a height of approximately 700ft, they exploded sending out white stars that slowly fell back into the sea. International regulations required that distress rockets were to be sent up 'at short intervals'. Boxhall sent up his rockets at a rate of about one every five minutes. In the meantime, Quartermasters Rowe and Bright maintained their attempts at contacting by Morse lamp.

On board the stationary *Californian* the officers on watch saw the first of eight white rockets explode high in the night sky. Upon notifying Captain Lord, they were ordered to try to contact their 'mystery vessel' by Morse lamp. Lord did not wake up his radio operator nor did he come on to the bridge himself to investigate the situation. It has been suggested that these white rockets may have been mistaken for company signals, but in 1912 most company signals were coloured and it was a requirement that under no circumstances were they to be confused with distress rockets. Second Officer Stone on *Californian* was to say at the British Inquiry, 'A ship is not going to fire rockets at sea for nothing.'

It appears that the vessel seen from *Californian* stopped at the same time as *Titanic* and the list on the stricken vessel could explain why her lights apparently 'went out'.

The rockets fired by *Titanic* were seen from *Californian* and, apart from attempts to contact by Morse lamp, usually only used within a range of 5 or 6 miles, no further action was taken by either Lord or his officers.

The sighting of the 'mystery vessel' by *Californian* ended at the same time as the lights went out on *Titanic*, just before she sank.

It is unlikely that *Californian*, even if she had made immediately for *Titanic*, would have arrived in time to save any lives but the 'lack of action' remains.

Cyril Evans, the sole wireless operator on *Californian*, turned off his set and went to bed about ten minutes before *Titanic*'s collision with the iceberg. At 6.05 a.m. on Monday 15 April, Evans received a message (MSG) from Captain Gambell of *Virginian* that he took to Captain Lord: 'Titanic struck berg wants assistance urgent, ship sinking, passengers in boats lat 41.46 long 50.14. Gambell. Commander.'

Upon the arrival of *Californian* in Boston it was thought that her logbooks would provide all the answers. It was not to be.

The 'scrap log', written up by the officers on watch at the end of the period on duty, had disappeared altogether. Third Officer Groves is believed to have said that he did not know what had happened to it but suspected that it may have been thrown overboard. Chief Officer Stewart had completed the entry in the official logbook for the night of 14/15 April 1912. There was no mention of rockets or other vessels seen that night.

On the Cunarder *Carpathia* the sole Marconi operator, Harold Cottam, was also about to retire that Sunday night. In his own words: 'It was only a stretch of luck that I got the message at all.' He had turned on his apparatus in order to contact *Titanic* to see if they were aware that a number of messages were being transmitted to them. He received a CQD message: 'Come at once we have struck a berg.' Cottam took the message to his bridge and gave it to First Officer Dean who immediately took it to Captain Arthur Rostron. Rostron altered course and made full speed for the reported position.

Captain Smith must have despaired upon receiving the reply. Fifty-eight miles and four hours! His ship would have sunk prior to the arrival.

eight

EVACUATION

The British Board of Trade, in an 1894 ruling that had not been updated, required that all passenger vessels over 10,000 tons carry sixteen lifeboats. *Titanic*, at over 45,000 tons, complied with this government regulation by carrying sixteen lifeboats and four collapsible-sided lifeboats. These had a total capacity of 1,178 persons, representing approximately one-third of her capacity or just over half of those on board that night.

Alexander Carlisle of Harland and Wolff, being principally involved in the design of the Olympic-class liners, planned to fit sixteen sets of davits. With White Star Line's approval, Carlisle's ideas were submitted to the Welin Quadrant Davit Company. Their davits could accommodate anything between one and four boats per set. Offering this design for Board of Trade approval in March 1910, Welin stated that the ships would each carry thirty-two lifeboats, two side by side under each set of davits.

Carlisle left Harland and Wolff on 30 June 1910 but twice, in May and July 1911, told the Merchant Shipping Advisory Committee that he considered British ships were carrying insufficient lifeboats. The committee ignored his comments and their report recommended that the existing situation remain unchanged.

No amendment having been received, White Star Line, unwilling to encroach on deck space, allowed the two vessels to depart on their respective maiden voyages with only one lifeboat under each set of davits. As such, despite being fitted with davits that could accommodate up to sixty-four boats, *Titanic* departed with sixteen wooden lifeboats, each supplied with oars, in two groups of four on each side. They were numbered 1 to 16, even numbers to port and odd to starboard. The forward boats, 1 and 2, on each side were classed as emergency cutters and swung out in preparedness.

The fourteen large wooden lifeboats each accommodated sixty-five persons and the two cutters forty persons each. These boats were lowered by hand with ropes threaded through block and tackle. The additional four collapsible-sided boats (A to D), each with a capacity of forty-seven persons, were stored at the forward end of the boat deck to be launched from the davits vacated by the cutters.

Shortly after departing Southampton it was Murdoch's responsibility to allocate members of the crew to lifeboat stations. The lists were placed in the relevant departments for perusal but it seems many of the crew either did not see or did not bother to look at them. On transatlantic crossings it was usual to have a boat drill for crew on a Sunday, but the drill for Sunday 14 April was cancelled, resulting in the crew of *Titanic* being unprepared for the task ahead of them. Needless to say, there had not been a passenger boat drill.

Smith, on the bridge awaiting Andrews' verdict and despite knowing that the damage to his ship was serious, still did not believe that *Titanic* would sink. Once that became known it would take some time for the terrible news to circulate. Aware that his ship carried lifeboats for just half of those on board, it must have been difficult for Smith to accept the situation himself let alone impart the news to his officers. Some were never told that the ship had less than two hours left afloat or that *Carpathia* was on her way. Boxhall, on the way back to the bridge after his investigation, alerted his off-duty fellow officers Pitman, Lowe and Lightoller.

Lightoller was told that the mailroom was flooding, indicating that the damage was serious. In fact, at that moment, the postal workers, all five of whom lost their lives, were hard at work hauling nearly 200 bags of registered mail away from the advancing water from F to, ultimately, C deck. The mail storage room on G deck, over 20ft above the keel, was flooded by midnight.

At a quarter past midnight only a few were aware of the situation and, despite the instruction for the crew to ready the lifeboats, an order to get the passengers off the vessel had not yet been issued. It seems that, to avoid panic, news of the drama was passed from crew member to crew member with only the occasional passenger being told.

Forty-five minutes after the collision things began to move more quickly. The bow had dipped some 20ft into the sea and the noise of the escaping steam continued to require that messages be conveyed by hand signals. Despite the fact that lifeboats had been readied, it still required Lightoller to 'nudge' Smith into action and issue the order for the crew to start filling them with women and children as quickly as possible and getting them away.

Hichens, who had been at the wheel at the time of the collision, heard Smith give the order to get the passengers on deck with their life belts on around this time. Purser McElroy and his team of stewards and stewardesses then began the task of waking the passengers, advising them to get dressed warmly and proceed to the open decks. This work was still ongoing as the lifeboats, having been uncovered, were released from their deck holdings, in some cases provisioned, and swung out on their davits.

Passengers now began appearing on the boat deck. The deafening noise of the escaping steam, as well as the bitter cold of the night air, forced many back inside the ship, and the entrance to the forward staircase at boat deck level became quite crowded, anxiety already showing on many faces.

More and more crew members, many still unaware of the seriousness of the situation, began turning up, including lookouts Hogg and Evans, who had relieved Lee and Fleet in the crow's nest at midnight. They had nothing to do any more as their ship had stopped.

As the forward parts of the ship flooded, third-class single male passengers, firemen and greasers all began moving to escape the rising water.

The passengers already on the boat deck, and many more joining them as the stewards and stewardesses worked their way through the cabins, began to be aware of the slightly sloping deck. This, added to the fact that the lifeboats had been uncovered and swung out, and that they were with lifejackets on, only increased the sense of unease. The anxiety was slight, however, and the majority of the passengers were still treating the situation with some humour.

The command to fill the boats was received at about 12.25 a.m., forty-five minutes after the collision with the iceberg.

After a lifeboat had been uncovered, it was necessary to ensure that the plug was in place, oars were aboard, the rudder was fitted and the ropes were coiled ready to lower the boat to the sea. Seamen on each davit would pay out the falls simultaneously, thus ensuring that the lifeboat would descend on an even keel.

Prior to being filled, the boat would be swung out and then lowered to the boat deck or, in some cases, the promenade deck below.

Murdoch took charge of the odd-numbered starboard boats and Lightoller the even-numbered port boats. Each of the two officers was not necessarily involved in the lowering of every boat on his side but was assisted by fellow officers and seamen. The numbers of seamen available became more critical as each lifeboat departed. The situation was not helped when Lightoller sent seven men below to open the side gangway doors, facilitating the boarding of more passengers when the half-empty boats reached the water. They were not seen again.

Murdoch, allegedly, applied a policy of 'women and children first' when loading his boats. If, at the time of lowering away, there were no more women or children willing to board, he would usually allow men into the boat.

Lightoller adopted 'women and children only' as his policy. Therefore, on his side of the deck, men were denied boarding even if there were spaces available and no women or children were around.

Most lifeboats departed with plenty of places remaining. Some of those responsible for loading and lowering away were concerned that a fully loaded lifeboat might buckle, despite the fact that the boats had been tested at Belfast filled to capacity. It should be remembered, however, that there was only just time to launch the lifeboats that *Titanic* did carry. It appears that those responsible for loading the boats were more concerned with getting them away as quickly as possible rather than delaying the departure looking for willing occupants.

Many passengers were initially reluctant to board the lifeboats as few were aware that *Titanic* was actually going to sink. Despite the slightly downward-sloping deck, the ship was on an even keel, warm and well lit. To exchange this comfort for the perils of an open boat and be lowered nearly 70ft down to a freezing black sea seemed unthinkable. Many of the women were also loath to leave their husbands during that early period.

The crew responsible for filling and lowering the boats believed also that boats could be filled from the gangway doors in the sides of the ship after they had released their falls.

Passengers, and in many cases crew, were unaware that *Titanic* carried insufficient lifeboats for all on board and, even if the light in the distance did not offer hope of rescue, they thought they could always get away if necessary in a later boat.

The water was by now entering the ship at a much greater rate than the pumps could possibly handle.

As preparations for evacuation were being made, the stokers and firemen down below were desperately trying to extinguish the fires and stop the build-up of steam, the noise of which was causing such havoc up top as it escaped through the safety valves on the funnels. Prior to the lowering of the first lifeboat the fires were put out, the noise ceased and stokers began to appear on the outer decks.

Only after the cessation of the noise did the passengers and crew realise that the band had begun to play. It is not known how many of the ship's eight-man band played that night as they were all lost, but it appears that they began playing in the forward first-class entrance on the boat deck.

Initially the music was light, consisting of ragtime and waltzes. Some believe that this may have instilled into the passengers a feeling that all was well, thus contributing to the loss of life. It is not known exactly when the band stopped playing but many of the survivors would comment that the music continued throughout the disaster but changed to a more serious content towards the end. The brave actions of the band that night ensured their place in history as heroes.

A greater proportion of the third-class passengers lost their lives in the sinking than in the other two classes, despite a couple of attempts by stewards to bring groups of women and children to the safety of the boat deck. It was difficult to persuade women and children to leave their husbands and fathers and accompany a perfect stranger out of areas to which they had become accustomed over the last five days. Many of the third-class passengers, only just under half of whom spoke English as their native language, would not be parted from their possessions and the network of narrow corridors soon became blocked by boxes, cases and packages. The signs directing passengers to safety were only in English and it seems that very little effort was made to keep the hundreds of third-class passengers informed, most of whom were unaware that the ship was sinking.

Those who were not prepared just to wait until being told what to do took the initiative to try to make it to the lifeboats. It is they, it seems, who came across barriers in some cases. Members of the crew locked some gates after groups of passengers had passed through and some were left open. It does seem, however, that there were occasions upon which locked barriers confronted third-class passengers.

Once escaping third-class passengers reached the boat deck, the women and children amongst them had no difficulty in boarding those few lifeboats that were still available. However, many third-class men, women and children congregated patiently in the general and smoking rooms to wait for instructions that never came.

The first lifeboat to leave was forward starboard No. 7 at 12.40 a.m., the filling and lowering of which was supervised by Murdoch and Lowe, who told the crew to stand off a short distance from the ship. With passengers reluctant to leave, the lifeboat departed with twenty-eight aboard over half of whom were men, including three crewmen, Hogg, Jewell and Weller.

Murdoch and Lowe then turned their attention to lifeboat 5. At the last moment Third Officer Pitman was ordered by Murdoch to take charge. Initially reluctant to go, Pitman felt that he could do more on board but he was aboard lifeboat 5 as it descended at 12.43 a.m. with thirty-six people. Pitman was asked to stand off and be prepared to come alongside, if hailed, to take on more passengers. It was at this time that Murdoch is believed to have said, 'Goodbye, Good Luck to you', as he shook Pitman's hand. When the ship sank Pitman was keen to return and collect survivors but, persuaded by the protestations of his passengers, he remained where he was.

Passengers still reticent to leave, Murdoch and Lowe moved forward to lifeboat 3, which was lowered away at 12.55 a.m. Several of the thirty-two aboard were firemen who had come up on deck after their jobs were made unnecessary down below. Seaman George Moore was put in charge. It seems No. 3 had intended to collect more passengers from A deck below, but, with the windows of that promenade deck closed, she continued her descent to the sea.

The first boat to be lowered on the port side was No. 8 at 1 a.m. Captain Smith assisted Wilde and Lightoller in filling No. 8 and again the officers found it difficult to persuade women and children to take to the boat, which was lowered away with twenty-five people aboard. Smith ordered Able Seaman Jones to row towards the light in the distance.

Having dispatched lifeboats 7, 5 and 3, Murdoch and Lowe moved forward to emergency cutter 1. Again they had difficulty in finding sufficient passengers willing to board and, at 1.05 a.m., the lifeboat was lowered away with her capacity of forty occupied by five passengers and seven crew. Lookout George Symons, in charge, was ordered to stand off and return when called.

The sixth lifeboat to leave, the second from the port side, was No. 6. Despite being amongst the least filled of the boats, she is famous primarily for her occupants. Smith and Lightoller put Quartermaster Hichens in charge, assisted by lookout Frederick Fleet who had been the first to see the iceberg. Short of seamen, having lost the seven dispatched below, Lightoller asked amongst the passengers for assistance. Canadian first-class passenger Major Arthur Peuchen lowered himself down the falls and became probably the only adult male passenger allowed by Lightoller to enter a lifeboat. Lightoller has said that it was now that he noticed the ship was 'severely down by the head'. Even so, he had great difficulty convincing women passengers to leave. One who was persuaded was Mrs J.J. Brown of Denver, later referred to as 'The Unsinkable Molly Brown'.

Finally, at 1.10 a.m., lifeboat 6 with twenty-three aboard was lowered away. Hichens remained steadfastly at the tiller and failed to help with the rowing, then later refused to return to the scene. He ignored Captain Smith's call to return, fearing that the boat would become overcrowded.

With most of the first-class women and children away, the ship severely down at the head and just over an hour to go before she sank, it was no longer difficult to persuade passengers to leave. Moody lowered No. 16 away from the port side with fifty-three aboard, amongst them stewardess Violet Jessop who had been aboard *Olympic* on the occasion of the collision with the Royal Navy cruiser HMS *Hawke*. She would later be aboard the third ship of the class, *Britannic*, when she sank as a hospital ship in 1916. Moody put Master-at-Arms Bailey in charge, having ordered him down the falls at the last minute.

As Moody was lowering No. 16 away at 1.20 a.m., Lowe, Wilde and Lightoller were trying to control the increasing number of anxious passengers around No. 14. Some men did attempt to rush this boat and were held off by Lowe, who fired his pistol along the side of the ship, and Seaman Joseph Scarrott, who warded them off with the lifeboat's tiller. The situation on board was growing tense and some women were being separated from their husbands and forcibly directed to the boats. As Lowe and Moody began handling lifeboats 14 and 16, Lowe mentioned that several had gone without an officer and Moody selflessly suggested that Lowe take command of No. 14 and that he would 'get in another boat'. Lowe joined his colleague Scarrott in No. 14 at 1.25 a.m., having disentangled one of the falls that had caused the boat to stop about 5ft above the sea. Sixth Officer James Moody, looking down on lifeboats 14 and 16 as they rowed away, would be the only junior officer to lose his life that night.

Wilde and Lightoller then continued forward on the port side and began loading No. 12. Stewards looked for women on both the boat and promenade decks but, in spite of this, lifeboat 12 was lowered away at 1.30 a.m. with forty-two aboard. Seaman John Poingdestre, in charge, was one of only two men in the boat.

Lifeboat 9, aft on the starboard side, had been ready for lowering for some time but several members of the crew had been diverted to the port side to manage the anxious crowds gathering around the aft boats. Murdoch and Moody ordered lifeboat 9 away with about forty on board at 1.30 a.m. – the same time that No. 12 was leaving the port side – and at the tiller was Seaman George McGough. Some ten minutes prior to No. 9's departure, many of the men working below had been free to leave, thus seven other members of the crew joined McGough. Once afloat the occupants noticed that *Titanic*, despite being ablaze with light, was dramatically down at the bow; they pulled away hard to escape any possible suction should she go down.

Murdoch then moved aft to the next lifeboat on the starboard side, No. 11. Moody was ordered down to A (promenade) deck to load the boat and Murdoch stayed on the boat deck to supervise the lowering. Some men in the crowd looked as if they might try to get in the boat and Murdoch had to point out that it was women and children first. After this warning, and despite the growing crowd, there were no further incidents and lifeboat 11 was lowered away at 1.35 a.m. with fifty occupants and Seaman Sidney Humphreys in charge.

Murdoch also lowered the last two starboard boats, Nos 13 and 15, to A deck, and Moody supervised the loading from there. Dr Washington Dodge, one of the occupants of lifeboat 13, later reported: 'We were in semi-darkness on the Boat Deck', and, 'We only knew what was going on about us within a radius of possibly forty feet'. It was becoming increasingly obvious that *Titanic* was sinking and time was running out fast. A considerable number of third-class passengers, until now patiently waiting on the aft well deck, began to appear on the boat deck. The build-up of passengers was greater on the port side and, having seen that Moody was nearly finished loading the two boats from A deck, Murdoch left to go and assist on the opposite side of the deck.

Lifeboat 13, Leading Fireman Frederick Barrett in charge, was lowered away at 1.40 a.m. with fifty-five people aboard. This was still less than her capacity of sixty-five and the figure was only reached when, no women being available at the time, several men were invited to board. Amongst the occupants was second-class passenger Lawrence Beesley, whose book, *The Loss of the SS Titanic*, published in June 1912, became one of the most dependable survivor accounts of the disaster.

As No. 13 reached the water, a condenser discharge from the side of the ship, which had also caused problems with No. 11's departure, pushed the boat aft until its falls were stretched tight. No. 13 was held directly under No. 15, which was lowered away a minute later at 1.41 a.m. The occupants of No. 13 shouted up to the seamen on the boat deck, Murdoch having left by this time, but their cries went unheard. The release mechanism of the falls could not be made to work so, at the last minute, a knife was produced and used to sever both ropes; No. 13 moved away just before No. 15 dropped into the vacated space.

After the crew had unlocked the small gates that had prevented the third-class passengers from accessing B deck, Steward Hart led a group of women and children to the safety of lifeboat 15 and joined them in the lifeboat.

As lifeboat 15 was lowered away, with Fireman Frank Dymond in charge and sixty-eight aboard, a list to port became noticeable. The occupants heard the cries of those in No. 13 and added their voices to the calls to those on the boat deck to stop lowering. Lifeboat 15 would be the only one of the sixteen wooden lifeboats that carried more than its capacity as it departed.

With all the starboard lifeboats away, the crew dealt with the last remaining boats on the port side. Emergency cutter 2 had been boarded by a considerable number of crewmen but Wilde, who had been looking for women to occupy his boat, and Smith ordered the men out and began to board those women that could be found. Finally, at 1.45 a.m., lifeboat 2 was lowered away. There were seventeen people in a boat with a capacity of forty. It should be pointed out that lifeboat 2 was the farthest away from the third-class men, women and children who were just beginning to appear and was also the nearest to the water.

Just prior to lifeboat 2's departure, Boxhall was ordered to take charge by Smith. He took with him a box of green flares and joined the one other seaman.

There were now only two large wooden lifeboats and the four collapsibles remaining, with just over half an hour to go before the ship sank and over 1,700 still on board.

By the time Murdoch, having left lifeboats 13 and 15 to be lowered unsupervised, arrived at lifeboat 10 it was still on the deck and had to be fitted into the davits, prepared for launch and lowered level to the boat

Sheet music from the Hebrew Publishing Co. in New York. Isidor and Ida Straus are shown above a naïve image of *Titanic* sinking. He was a founder member of Macy's department store in New York. Mrs Straus opted to stay with her husband rather than take a seat in a lifeboat and they perished together.

deck for loading. The list to port, slightly noticeable at the time of No. 15's departure, had now increased to about 10 degrees, which meant that lifeboat 10 swung over 2ft away from the side of the boat deck. Most of the escapees had to negotiate this gap as they boarded but, without incident, No. 10 departed with fifty-seven aboard at 1.50 a.m., Seaman Edward Buley in charge.

Lightoller's intention, earlier that night, had been to lower No. 4 and board it from the promenade (A) deck. Several of the more prominent passengers had been instructed to proceed to that deck prior to boarding No. 4. First, it was necessary to wind down the windows of that part of the promenade deck, which had been glass-enclosed. The crank to open the windows could not be found so Lightoller, having dispatched stewards to search for the missing crank, turned to the next boats aft.

It was at this time that the famous incident of Mr and Mrs Straus took place. Mrs Straus was heard to say, 'No, I will not be separated from my husband; as we have lived so will we die together.' Upon hearing the suggestion that the elderly Mr Straus be allowed to join his wife in a boat, he is believed to have replied, 'No, I do not want any distinction in my favour which is not granted to others.' Later Mrs Straus gave her fur coat to her maid Ellen Bird and waved her off in lifeboat 8.

Nearly ninety minutes later, the crank handles having been found, Lightoller began loading No. 4. In order to counteract the effects of the list to port, he secured the boat to the coaling wire that ran alongside A deck. There was a gap, however, and it became necessary to almost throw the female passengers across after they had arrived at the opened window by means of piled-up deckchairs.

In the meantime, the group of passengers had, after being ordered up to the boat deck and then back down to the promenade deck, been patiently waiting and becoming more aware of the approaching danger. Lightoller, only allowing women and children into his boats, then requested that the women board No. 4. Mrs Widener, Mrs Ryerson and Mrs Astor all bade farewell to their husbands, never to see them again. Lifeboat 4, capacity sixty-five, was lowered away at 1.50 a.m., half an hour before the ship sank and with thirty aboard. Two additional seamen were ordered down the falls, as Lightoller felt that there were too few to man the boat, and Quartermaster Walter Perkis was put in charge. As lifeboat 4 reached the sea, water was pouring through the open forward portholes and the liner's propellers were half out of the water.

nine

FATAL NIGHT

As the last large wooden lifeboat pulled away, it was becoming increasingly obvious to the hundreds remaining on board that their ship was sinking. The initial mood of light-hearted optimism had been replaced by one of alarm. The black, calm surface of the sea was slowly creeping nearer to the ship's name on the bow as the slant of the deck increased downwards. The last few aft lifeboats had been lowered away with many more aboard than their earlier counterparts.

In the minutes before 2 a.m. Captain Smith had hailed the half-empty lifeboats already afloat demanding that they return, but most of the boats did not come back, fearing suction as the ship went down or claiming that they were already too full. Boxhall, in No. 2, did, however, obey and began to slowly row back to the stern by which time nearly 30,000 tons of seawater had entered the vessel.

Events now occurred at a frantic pace as many third-class passengers arrived on the boat deck. Some of these people had faced locked barriers, but not all: the majority of the third class had access to the open deck. As less than half spoke English and the boat deck was in the first- and second-class area of the ship, many arrived late at the now-empty davits.

Between loading and launching the port boats, Lightoller had taken the opportunity to gauge the degree of sinking. By taking a quick look down the well of the emergency spiral staircase, leading down to C deck, he could see the rising seawater at its foot.

Up until now the loading and lowering of the sixteen lifeboats had taken place calmly and in an orderly fashion. The male passengers had not forced their way on to lifeboats, but, in most cases, had been either invited or ordered to board, and most people had not known that the ship was sinking at the time.

Not many postcards of the time depicted such a realistic scene. (W. Pearson)

W. Pearson.   WRECK OF S.S. "TITANIC," APRIL, 1912.

Just after the disaster, postcard publishers doctored any image that they could find. This was originally *Titanic* fitting out at Belfast. (Ann St)

The Ill-fated "S. S. TITANIC" Wrecked April 15th, 1912

ANN. ST. BADGE & NOVELTY CO   21-23 ANN ST. NEW YORK

As water began to flow on to the forward well deck, those aboard realised that, not only was the ship sinking, but also all the lifeboats had gone. All but the four collapsibles.

In addition to her sixteen lifeboats, *Titanic* carried four Englehardt collapsible lifeboats. Each was capable of carrying forty-seven persons and located at the forward end of the boat deck, two (C and D) on the deck inboard of the cutters and A and B on the roof of the officers' quarters behind the bridge. After the emergency boats had left it was necessary for the crew to bring the davits back in, hook up the collapsible boat, raise the canvas sides and swing it out in preparation for loading – a much more difficult operation than with the main boats.

The first, C, was fitted into the davits vacated by cutter 1, loaded and lowered away by Wilde and Murdoch at 2 a.m. In charge was Quartermaster George Rowe, who had earlier been on the stern docking bridge and ordered forward with a supply of emergency rockets. It was reported by some that shots were fired to deter a rush of male passengers or crew. Having called in vain for more women passengers, Murdoch ordered the boat away with forty-one aboard. Just at that moment two male passengers entered the boat as it began its descent, one of whom was, controversially, J. Bruce Ismay, Chairman and Managing Director of the White Star Line. It is unknown whether he was invited or ordered in, or whether he took the boat on his own initiative.

As collapsible C was ordered away, the forward well deck was awash but, as she reached the water, it was already submerged and water was on the forward promenade (A) deck.

Collapsible D, fitted into the davits vacated by lifeboat 2, was loaded and lowered away at 2.05 a.m. by Wilde and Lightoller. It became necessary for crewmen to link arms, preventing any rush for this last lifeboat, and only women and children were permitted through.

Much has been said about the heroic actions of the engineers who stayed at their posts until the ship went down. It is believed, however, that most of those men were on deck as the ship sank, but, nevertheless, none survived and they did ensure that power to the ship, albeit lessening towards the end, was supplied until the eventual sinking.

Many of the officers, including Captain Smith, were armed but most witnesses to shooting, or the possible suicide of an officer, either perished in the disaster or had evidence that was too hazy to be reliable.

We shall never be completely sure as to the behaviour of Smith that night but can only imagine that the man must have been in a considerable state of shock. It does appear that he was initially reluctant to begin lowering away the lifeboats and may have pinned his hopes on 'the light in the distance'. It seems that he stayed in the area of the bridge throughout the disaster and assisted in the lowering of lifeboats 2, 6 and 8.

Titanic departing Southampton becomes *Titanic* at sea!

THE WHITE STAR LINER "TITANIC."
Foundered on her Maiden Voyage, 15th April, 1912.
Tonnage, 45,000 Tons.   Length, 882½ feet.   Breadth, 92½ feet.

THE ILL-FATED S. S. "*Titanic*" OF THE WHITE STAR LINE WHICH SANK ON HER MAIDEN TRIP APRIL 15TH 1912 WITH A LOSS OF OVER 1500 SOULS.

Even Cunard's *Mauretania* doubled as *Titanic* in the rush to get postcards to the public. The only similarity here is four funnels!

He kept checking with Boxhall as to whether there had been any response from 'the light on the port bow' and also liaised with the wireless operators. Captain Smith and his officers, in many cases at the expense of their lives, ensured that all the lifeboats, except the two remaining collapsibles, were loaded and successfully lowered away, thus saving the lives of many.

The ship's designer would have been the first to know that the ship was going to sink. Thomas Andrews had not felt the impact of the iceberg but, after his inspection of the damage caused, it was down to him to let Smith know that the vessel could not be saved. Later he was seen persuading crew to wear their lifejackets, leading passengers to the lifeboats, informing those he could trust and even, towards the end, throwing deck chairs into the sea. However, at the last, he was seen in the first-class smoking room, lifejacket discarded, staring at the painting of Plymouth Harbour.

In the 'legend' of *Titanic* there are constant references to the ship's orchestra 'playing until the end'. This is very probably true but it is unlikely that they played out on the open deck, where the freezing temperature would have made the playing of stringed instruments extremely difficult. What is more likely is that they played in the warmth and shelter of the top of the first-class forward grand staircase on the boat deck. Neither shall we know what the last piece of music played by those brave men was or whether *Nearer my God to Thee*, which has three different musical interpretations, was ever played at all. The Methodist tune to *Nearer my God to Thee*, *Propior Deo*, is believed to have been a favourite of bandleader Wallace Hartley, however.

For the occupants of those lifeboats at sea it was much more obvious that *Titanic* was sinking. Line after line of portholes was slipping under as the bow submerged and the starboard propeller became visible as the list to port increased to about 10 degrees. Most directed their attention to getting as far away as possible, fearing suction as the ship went down.

After the first two collapsibles had departed, it was obvious that there would not be time to get the remaining two into the davits and the hundreds remaining on board bravely awaited the dreadful final moments.

At about 2.15 a.m. the forward part of the ship took a slight but definite plunge. This was probably caused by one of the forward bulkheads giving way, the resulting wave travelling up the deck and sweeping away all it encountered. The crow's nest, located high in the forward mast, was by this time level with the surface of the Atlantic.

Those passengers and crew still on the boat deck began to move aft as the wave swept along the deck. Panic set in as their way became blocked by hundreds of third-class passengers still in the aft well deck, who

The Musician Hero of the Titanic
which foundered April 14th, 1912.

Near er my God to Thee, Near er to Thee.

¡MAS CERCA DE TI, DIOS MIO!
(NEARER, MY GOD, TO THEE!)
PLEGARIA
Ejecutada por la banda, en el trágico momento del hundimiento del TITANIC
Versión Castellana
Arreglo para Canto y Piano por
A. S. ARISTA

Left: Wallace Hartley's body was recovered and returned to Colne in Lancashire for a funeral that was attended by thousands.

Above: Sheet music from Argentina illustrated with a graphic depiction of the sinking on the front cover.

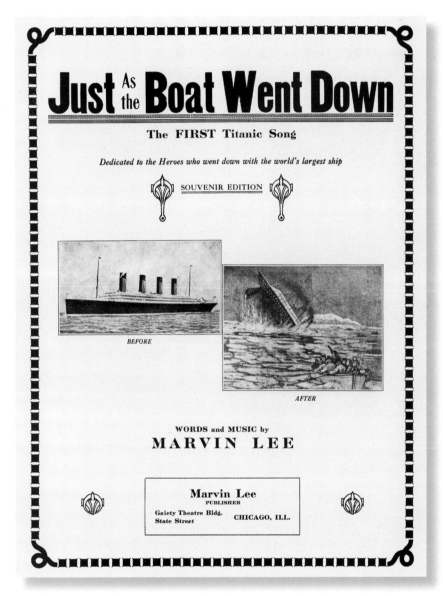

Just As the Boat Went Down

The FIRST Titanic Song

Dedicated to the Heroes who went down with the world's largest ship

SOUVENIR EDITION

BEFORE

AFTER

WORDS and MUSIC by
MARVIN LEE

Marvin Lee
PUBLISHER
Gaiety Theatre Bldg.
State Street   CHICAGO, ILL.

Sheet music, a popular medium at the time, depicting the end of *Titanic*.

must have long given up any hope of access to the lifeboats or indeed survival.

Meanwhile, in the Marconi room, operator Jack Phillips was continuing to send out the distress message when Smith made his penultimate visit, telling the two men that water was filling the engine room and the dynamos could not last for much longer. Phillips, during a brief exploratory visit outside, returned and told his assistant Bride that there was a considerable list to port, the lights were losing their brilliance and he might not have the power to transmit much longer. At about 2.10 a.m. Smith made his last visit and released the two men, saying, according to Bride, 'Men you have done your full duty. You can do no more. Abandon your cabin … I release you. That's the way of it at this kind of time.' With that, the two men left the cabin.

It is thought that the last message sent from *Titanic* was at 2.12 a.m. but, with the loss of power, this message would have been very faint.

Over the last hour the supply of steam to the dynamos had lessened to such a degree that, not only was the transmitter affected, but the ship's lights were growing dimmer and beginning to glow red.

With the crew desperately trying to free the two remaining collapsible boats, A and B, *Titanic* began her final moments.

Collapsible A fell the right way up on to the boat deck but there was no time to get her canvas sides fully raised. The on-rushing sea swept out most of the occupants and, as it floated off, others scrambled aboard. About twenty successfully climbed into the boat but, during the night, several succumbed to the knee-deep freezing water.

Collapsible B had fallen on to the boat deck upside down and was washed off as the ship began to sink. The upturned boat was washed away from those struggling in the freezing water by the fall of the forward funnel, which, having just missed the boat, swept it away from the mass of humanity. About thirty people were able to climb aboard the upturned hull, among them Lightoller and Bride.

Inevitably, the falling funnel killed a considerable number as it hit the surface of the sea. Up until this moment *Titanic* had offered her passengers and crew a reasonably level base from which to send lifeboats away, but all this was now to change. Many of those on board began to head for the 'security' of the stern, rising steadily out of the water and revealing the three giant propellers.

TITANIC DISASTER APRIL 15TH 1912
1.635 PERISH AT SEA

① CAPTAIN SMITH. ② PHILLIPS THE HERO OPERATOR.
3. RESCUING A PASSENGER. Bonner, Arcade House, Whitley Bay.

Overdramatic illustrations were often produced, such as on this postcard. Note the sea birds, daylight and is that land on the left?

Just after two audible cracks, all the ship's lights were extinguished and the vessel began to break in two between the third and fourth funnels, which were unable to stay in position as the stay-wires could not hold them at such an unnatural angle and they also fell: the third funnel forward and the fourth aft funnel backwards. The stern, which initially had been pulled upwards by the sinking bow, had, since separating, fallen back almost on to an even keel.

Some maintain that the ship was built using inferior material and that is why she broke apart. This is not the case and *Titanic* split only when her hull was stressed to breaking point at the final moments of her sinking.

As the stern section, to which hundreds of people were still clinging, began to fill with water, it started to rise to almost a perpendicular position. Mercifully the darkness spared those in the lifeboats the horror of witnessing the last terrible minutes. Those few survivors, who were on board at the time, were more concerned with saving their own lives than taking note of what was happening around them. Some of those in the lifeboats described the up-ended stern as being like an enormous black finger against the sky. A rumbling sound spread across the ocean and slowly the remainder of the vessel disappeared from view with very little suction and hardly a ripple.

It was 2.20 a.m. on Monday 15 April 1912 at location 41 degrees 43.5 N, 49 degrees 56.8 W. The two major pieces of the vessel lie about 750 yards apart at a depth of nearly 2½ miles. The aerodynamic dimensions of the bow sent it to the bottom relatively intact in the space of about six minutes, reaching a speed of nearly 20 knots. The stern, however, is a complete mess. Decks are peeled back upon one another and, upon contact with the seabed, there was shattering damage.

The wreck location, discovered by Dr Robert Ballard and his team in 1985, was considerably in error when compared to that originally given out by the wireless operators in their distress signals of 1912, as they were given the incorrect location by Boxhall.

Those in the lifeboats were unprepared for what came next. The cries filled the air of hundreds of men, women and children, most wearing lifejackets, who were now suffering the agonies of the freezing water. This was in addition to the horrors of the darkness and being amidst hundreds struggling for their lives and calling for assistance that was not to come.

The temperature of the water was 28°F. Clinging to wreckage would not have saved a person as it would be necessary to get one's whole being out of the water. The first effects would be panic and shock. Unconsciousness, caused by hypothermia, swiftly followed. Within forty-five minutes the majority of the nearly 1,500 people would have lost their lives but were still held afloat by their lifejackets.

A terrible choice faced those in the lifeboats: to go back and attempt rescue or not? There was room in the boats for more than 1,100 people; only 700 seats were occupied. Two lifeboats were instrumental in saving lives: No. 4 – one of the last to leave the ship – was nearby as *Titanic* went down and rescued about eight from the water. She then joined lifeboats 10, 12 and collapsible D. Lowe, in lifeboat 14, transferred thirty-three of his passengers to these boats and returned with a volunteer crew. He arrived at the scene about an hour after the sinking but was only able to rescue three men alive.

Lifeboat 4, in addition to her own occupants, took about ten from Lowe's No. 14 and later that night rescued around twelve people standing on upturned collapsible B. Launched initially only half full, lifeboat 4 would eventually reach the rescue ship with nearly sixty on board.

It is in connection with collapsible B that we last hear of Captain Smith. It is possible that he jumped overboard as *Titanic* sank and eventually reached the upturned lifeboat. Some of those standing on the boat in the darkness believe that they heard the captain call out and swim away offering words of encouragement after being denied boarding.

Quartermaster Hichens, at the tiller of half-empty lifeboat 6, ignored the pleas of his fellow occupants and refused to return to the scene of the sinking. Many of his actions in the boat that night were questionable.

As the cries of those in the water died away, the occupants of the lifeboats awaited daylight or rescue. Few were even aware of the existence of a rescue vessel.

Those in the boats represented 62 per cent of the first-class passengers, 41 per cent of second class, 25 per cent of third class and 24 per cent of the crew. A considerably high proportion – 68 per cent – of the deck crew survived, as it was they who were sent away manning the lifeboats and assisting with the rowing, but this was not reflected in other departments. Twenty-two per cent of the engineering crew survived and only 19 per cent of the victualling department.

Aboard the stationary steamer *Californian*, Captain Lord was informed that the lights of the ship they had been watching had disappeared.

White Star Line used this illustration on the cover of its brochure
advertising the two new super liners.

THE NEW WHITE STAR LINER "TITANIC."

45,000 tons gross register.   66,000 tons displacement.   Built by Harland & Wolff, Belfast ; launched October 20, 1910.
Accommodation, 2500 passengers and a crew of 860.   Speed 21 knots.   Estimated cost, £1,500,000.
The "Olympic" is 100 feet longer and 12,500 tons more than the Cunard leviathans.   The following are the dimensions, etc., of the great vessel :

Length over all	882 ft. 9 in.	Distance from top of funnel to keel	175 ft. 0 in.
Breadth over all	92 ft. 6 in.	Number of steel decks	11
Breadth over boat deck	94 ft. 0 in.	Number of water-tight bulkheads	15
Height from bottom of keel to boat deck	97 ft. 4 in.	Rudder weighs	100 tons.
Height from bottom of keel to top of captain's house	105 ft. 7 in.	Stern frame, rudder and brackets	280 tons.
		Each anchor	15 tons.
Height of funnels above casing	72 ft. 0 in.	Bronze Propellor	22 tons.
Height of funnels above boat deck	81 ft. 6 in.	Launching weight	27,000 tons.

WALTON, PUBLISHER, BELFAST.

Originally published for *Olympic*, her name has been replaced by *Titanic* on the
top line only on this postcard! (Walton)

An early advertisement for traveller's cheques featuring either of the two new liners.

CUSTOM HOUSE AND SHIPYARDS, BELFAST

The imposing Custom House in Belfast (1856) with the large gantry and
crane at Harland and Wolff in the background.

NEW FLOATING CRANE, HARLAND & WOLFF'S, BELFAST.

The Benrather Floating Crane purchased from Germany for the construction of *Olympic* and *Titanic*. (Private collection)

The World's Greatest Gantry, in Harland & Wolff's North Shipyard, Belfast.

Titanic (left) and *Olympic*, in a more advanced state of construction, at Harland and Wolff.

Olympic returns to Belfast in 1912 for repairs. The last time the two vessels were together. (Original painting by Neil Egginton)

Titanic arrives at Berth 44, Southampton, at 1.15 a.m. on Thursday 4 April 1912. *Oceanic* and *New York* on the right at Berth 39. (Original painting by Neil Egginton)

Titanic quietly waits at the White Star Dock, Southampton. (Original painting by Neil Egginton)

The boat train and busy platform at Waterloo Station. Note the dog with the 'Collection Box' bottom left! (Misch & Co. / private collection)

On the way to the ship!

Titanic proceeds down Southampton Water after near collision. *New York* has already been warped into Berth 37. (Original painting by Simon Fisher)

CHERBOURG — Les Voyageurs qui vont s'embarquer, descendent du train spécial qui les amène devant la **Gare Maritime**

Passengers disembarking from the boat train at the Gare Maritime in Cherbourg. (Verschuere / private collection)

A delayed *Titanic* arrives at Cherbourg and awaits the tenders. (Original painting by Neil Egginton)

As dusk falls, *Titanic* embarks her passengers from the tenders at Cherbourg. (Original painting by
Neil Egginton)

Ireland and *America* approach a White Star liner at Queenstown.

A rare image of *Titanic* at sea.

North German Lloyd's *Frankfurt*, one of the first to receive the CQD signal. (W. Sander)

Titanic at sea on Sunday night. Note the ice in the water! (Original painting by Neil Egginton)

The crippled *Titanic*, excess steam pouring from her funnels, begins to settle by the bow. (Original painting by Simon Fisher)

Californian had fewer lifeboats than the vessel in this illustration.

The occupants of these lifeboats are somewhat more animated than they would have been in reality.

The arrival of "S. S. Carpathia" after the disaster - April 15t 1912

ATLANTIC TRANSPORT LINE.

MINNEWASKA

S.S. MINNEWASKA

Atlantic Transport's *Minnewaska* transmitted the list of surviving crew to the US from *Carpathia*.
(Tuck, Oilette)

The Most Appalling Disaster in Maritime History.

The White Star Liner "TITANIC," sunk on her maiden voyage off Cape Race, 15th April, 1912.

Publishers were quick to produce postcards after the disaster. This rare, coloured card carries the ship's
statistics on the reverse. (Valentine's)

ten

BY THE DAWN'S EARLY LIGHT

The 13,600-ton Cunard liner *Carpathia* departed New York on 11 April 1912 for Gibraltar and the Mediterranean. Carrying 728 passengers (128 first class, 50 second class and 550 third class), she was commanded by Captain Arthur Rostron, who had been at sea for almost twenty-seven years.

Her Marconi operator, Harold Cottam, a friend of Jack Phillips, had previously served on White Star Line's *Medic*, worked from morning to midnight and had been with Marconi for three years, earning £4 10s per month.

Unaware of the distress signals on the 14th, Cottam had just forwarded several messages for passengers on *Titanic* from the radio station at Cape Race. Phillips replied, 'Come at once. We have struck a berg. 41.46N, 50.14W. It's a CQD OM [Old Man].' The surprised Cottam asked if he should alert his captain. Phillips repeated, 'It's a CQD old man.' Within minutes *Carpathia* had turned north-west towards the distress position, Rostron having calculated that they were 58 miles away. His vessel's maximum speed was estimated to be 14 knots.

Cottam returned to his set and stayed in contact with Phillips, who was having difficulty hearing the incoming messages due to the noise of the released steam. Monitoring the messages, Cottam let Phillips know of anything he may have missed.

Rostron placed an additional two men, to act as lookouts, in the bow to aid the one man in the crow's nest, whilst on the bridge were now three officers and a quartermaster.

Eventually the noise of the escaping steam stopped but the two Marconi operators continued to stay in touch, despite the fact that the wireless on *Titanic* was gradually becoming weaker. It is believed that the last message heard by *Carpathia* was sent from *Titanic* at 1.57 a.m. with the words, 'Come quick; our engine room is filling up to the boilers.'

Phillips, having fired a controversial parting shot at the hapless wireless operator on board the German steamer *Frankfurt* – 'You are a fool. Keep out and do not interfere with our communications' – tried to let *Carpathia* know that they were leaving their cabin and abandoning ship. Bride later stated that he heard the band playing ragtime music as he left.

Carpathia, turning and making at top speed for the reported position, now became a hive of activity as Rostron's orders were put into action. All lifeboats were to be uncovered and swung out and all gangway doors were to be opened. The English doctor and assistants would remain in the first-class dining room, the Italian doctor and assistants in second class and Hungarian doctor and assistants in third class. Each doctor was to be fully equipped with medical supplies. Third-class passengers were to be kept out of their dining room and the open deck by stewards and the master-at-arms.

The purser's department, with the chief steward, were to receive the survivors with the help of the stewards directing them to their respective dining rooms and obtaining their names to be forwarded on by wireless as soon as possible. The chief steward was advised that all hands were to be called and coffee etc. was to be available to all the crew. Coffee, tea, soup etc. was also to be available in each dining saloon and blankets were to be located there, as well as in the gangways and in the boats that had been swung out. Stewards were to be placed in each alleyway to reassure their passengers enquiring about the noise and the upheaval.

Rostron's cabin and those of all the officers were to be given up and the smoking rooms, library and dining rooms were to be used to accommodate the survivors. Rostron wanted to ensure that all the rescued were cared for and immediate needs attended to, and this was to be managed with order, discipline and quietness to avoid confusion.

All the spare berths in third class were to be utilised for the survivors and all third-class passengers on *Carpathia* were to be grouped together.

Boatswain's chairs, pilot ladders and canvas ash bags for children were to be at each gangway. As an order was carried out each official had to report to Rostron on the bridge that everything was in readiness.

Meanwhile at the scene of the sinking, after the cries of the dying had faded away, the survivors sat and waited in the darkness. Boxhall in lifeboat 2 would occasionally light one of his green flares. Lowe in lifeboat 14, having returned from the scene of the disaster with only three or four rescued from the water, had raised his boat's mast and sail, and was the only one to do so.

The thirteen or so survivors in collapsible A, still standing up to their knees in freezing water, were unaware that they had been seen until they saw Lowe's sail approaching them. He began transferring them to his lifeboat.

Lightoller, balancing on upturned collapsible B, had periodically been using his officer's whistle to attract attention. The occupants of lifeboats 4 and 12 heard it and they approached and rescued the twenty-eight or so people standing on the bottom of the upturned lifeboat. Lifeboat 12, having rescued sixteen of those, eventually reached the rescue ship carrying nearly seventy people.

The first two lifeboats away, Nos 7 and 5, tied themselves together and about six of Pitman's passengers transferred to No. 7. He was joined in No. 5 by Crewman Olliver.

Lifeboat 3 attempted to row towards the light in the distance but eventually gave up. Similarly, lifeboat 8, with the Countess of Rothes at the tiller, despite rowing for 3 or 4 miles towards the light, abandoned the attempt.

After *Titanic* had gone down, the seven crew in emergency cutter 1 were dissuaded by the five passengers from returning to the scene to attempt any rescue.

Quartermaster Hichens at the tiller of half-empty lifeboat 6 ignored the pleas of his fellow occupants and refused to return to the scene of the sinking. His conduct, according to some, left much to be desired that night, with accusations of belligerency and threatening behaviour. Later that night, lifeboat 6 tied up to No. 16 and a member of the latter's crew was transferred to assist with the rowing.

Dawn was slowly breaking on the horizon and the sea became slightly choppy as a breeze began to spring up. The stars, which had been shining brilliantly throughout the night, began to fade and, as the sun began to rise, the occupants of the lifeboats saw the icebergs that surrounded them. About twenty-five were over 150ft high – and most people had not even been aware of their presence that preceding evening.

Carpathia raced through the night, her added lookouts peering ahead for any sight of *Titanic*. Rostron had calculated that it would take him about four hours to reach the scene, but the journey took half an hour less. The extra steam was created by all power being diverted to the boilers, and the vessel reached speeds of up to an incredible 17½ knots. During her race, *Carpathia* negotiated about six large icebergs. Later, Rostron is reported as saying: 'When day broke, I saw the ice I had steamed through during the night. I shuddered, and could only think that some other hand than mine was on the helm during that night.'

Had *Carpathia* not sighted Boxhall's green flares, she might have missed the lifeboats in the darkness and proceeded directly to the erroneous position. However, Rostron, having seen Boxhall's signals, ordered that rockets be fired at fifteen-minute intervals to reassure the passengers and crew on *Titanic* that help was on the way.

Carpathia arrived at the wreck site at about 4 a.m. ship's time, and lifeboat 2 was alongside by 4.10 a.m. As survivors began clambering aboard, Boxhall was taken directly to Rostron and informed him that *Titanic* had sunk.

Titanic lifeboats approach Cunard's *Carpathia* on Monday 15 April 1912. (Joseph Koehler)

Rescuing the 705 survivors of the Titanic, sunk off Halifax, April 15, 1912. 1,600 persons were drowned. Insurance loss, $14,500,000. Published by Joseph Koehler, 150 Park Row, N. Y.

The Carpathia was on her way to the Mediterranean with 200 passengers on board, when Capt. Rostron received the distress calls from the Titanic, fifty-six miles away.

"S. S. CARPATHIA,"

"TITANIC" LIFEBOAT ALONGSIDE "CARPATHIA"

J. W. Barker, Copyright.

Lifeboat 11, alongside *Carpathia*, begins unloading her passengers. (Barker)

Meanwhile, the occupants of the other lifeboats, seeing *Carpathia* stopped in the distance, began rowing towards salvation.

Titanic had been pointing in a northerly direction just before she sank and, as *Carpathia* approached from the south-south-east, the odd-numbered (starboard) lifeboats generally arrived first. Lifeboat 2 had rowed behind the stern of *Titanic* before she sank, hence being the first to arrive.

The first arrival came alongside with seventeen survivors. Just over half an hour later, at 4.45 a.m., lifeboat 1 arrived with twelve occupants. An hour later the nearly full collapsible C pulled alongside, at 5.45 a.m. After the forty-three survivors had clambered aboard, their boat was set adrift. Shortly afterwards, at 6 a.m., the thirty occupants of lifeboat 5 came aboard. Their boat had been tied up to lifeboat 7 during the night and thus it was this boat that discharged her thirty-four occupants next at 6.15 a.m. Lifeboats now began to arrive at frequent intervals. Also at 6.15 a.m., forty survivors from lifeboat 9 began to climb aboard, followed at 6.30 a.m. by fifty-five from lifeboat 13. Next to arrive was lifeboat 16, with fifty-two aboard, at 6.45am; she was followed, at 7 a.m., by the fifty aboard No. 11.

Several were too exhausted to climb rope ladders the short distance to the side gangway doors, so they were hoisted aboard with the aid of bosun's chairs, and canvas bags for the children.

As the crew of *Carpathia* assisted the survivors aboard, they took down their names and classes, and led them to the respective dining saloons, where they were given blankets and hot drinks.

Lowe's lifeboat 14 was the next to arrive at 7.15 a.m., with a mix of volunteer crew and passengers rescued from collapsible A, totalling some twenty-five people. Lifeboat 14 had been towing the thirty-five survivors in collapsible D, and the latter was the next to arrive, also at 7.15 a.m. No. 14 and D were set adrift after their occupants were safely aboard.

Thirty-two people were in lifeboat 3 as she pulled alongside at 7.30 a.m., followed by twenty-five in No. 8 at the same time. Carrying an estimated sixty-eight survivors, lifeboat 15 also arrived at 7.30 a.m., later to be set adrift with the next arrival: lifeboat 4, at 8 a.m., with sixty aboard.

"TITANIC" LIFEBOAT UNDER SAIL.

J. W. Barker, Copyright.

Copyright by Underwood & Underwood, N. Y.

Boat Load of "Titanic" Survivors Approaching the "Carpathia"

"TITANIC" LIFEBOAT APPROACHING "CARPATHIA"

J. W. Barker, Copyright.

Above left: Lifeboat 14 – the only boat to use her sail – approaches the rescue ship. (Barker)

Above: Collapsible D had been towed by lifeboat 14. (Underwood & Underwood)

Lifeboat 6, with oars stowed and Quartermaster Hichens still at the tiller, drifts towards *Carpathia*. (Barker)

Lifeboat 6, with Hichens still at the tiller, arrived alongside *Carpathia* with twenty-four occupants at 8 a.m. The fifty-five aboard No. 10 also came aboard at 8 a.m. The last lifeboat, No. 12, came alongside at about 8.15 a.m. Amongst her estimated sixty-nine occupants was Lightoller, having been rescued from collapsible B. He was the last survivor to board *Carpathia*. Many of the rescued were still leaning over the railings anxiously, searching for familiar faces. The number of occupants in each lifeboat is based on an estimated figure but it is generally accepted that there were 712 survivors. Upon boarding *Carpathia*, they were told that they would be able, without charge, to send Marconigrams to relatives; however, perhaps due to the volume required, it appears that many were not sent.

By about 8.30 a.m. all survivors and thirteen of the lifeboats had been taken aboard *Carpathia*; six of the boats were placed on the forward deck and seven carried under davits.

At 8.50 a.m. Rostron, satisfied that all lifeboats were accounted for, raised speed and headed towards New York.

As she sailed away, *Carpathia* was seen by *Californian* which, having been advised by *Mount Temple* that *Titanic* had sunk, had arrived on the scene and was asked by *Carpathia* to continue searching the wreckage. *Californian* left the site at about 11.20 a.m.

Trapped on the wrong side of a large field of ice lay *Mount Temple*, four hours and twenty minutes after turning round in response to the distress call. She sighted *Carpathia* on the other side of the ice field and later saw *Californian* in her vain search for more survivors.

Amongst the wreckage was the overturned hull of collapsible B.

Vessels chartered by the White Star Line recovered about 337 bodies. The cable ship *Mackay-Bennett* buried 116 at sea and returned to Halifax on 30 April with 190 aboard. Coffins were used for those bodies that were thought to be first class, and these were stacked on the open deck. The remaining bodies were placed below in sewn-up sacks. Six days later the *Minia* returned with fifteen bodies, two having been buried at sea. *Montmagny* and *Algerine* later returned to Halifax with four more bodies, having buried just one at sea.

CALIFORNIAN & CARPATHIA

Both vessels had been built in the UK in 1902, *Californian* by Caledon in Dundee and *Carpathia* by Swan Hunter in Newcastle.

The 6,223grt *Californian* was operated by the Leyland Line and, although primarily a cargo vessel, did provide passenger accommodation for thirty-five.

On 9 November 1915, *Californian* succumbed to a torpedo in the Mediterranean.

The 13,603grt *Carpathia* made her maiden voyage, for the Cunard Line in May 1903, from Liverpool to Boston calling at Queenstown, Ireland. Within a year she had been switched to Cunard's Mediterranean service from New York. It was on her way from New York to Fiume that she responded to *Titanic*'s distress call in 1912.

On 17 July 1918, whilst in convoy, she was sunk by three torpedoes west of Bishop's Rock. Five were killed in the initial explosion, but the escorting vessel HMS *Snowdrop* rescued 215 survivors.

eleven

CUNARD TO NEW YORK

Rostron, having made the decision to return to New York, was forced to sail approximately 56 miles off course before being able to negotiate the ice field. Whereas Halifax would have been nearer, his decision to head for New York was based on the fact that facilities there were better suited, not only for the survivors, but also for his own passengers. Additionally, he was now carrying too many for his on-board supplies to accommodate, were he to continue his journey to the Mediterranean.

Many of the survivors still held the false hope that other ships may have rescued their friends and relatives, but it was not until the arrival in New York that the awful truth became known.

Ernest Moore, Marconi operator on *Olympic*, which was making her way at top speed towards the distress position, made contact with Cottam on *Carpathia* early that Monday afternoon. Rostron told Captain Haddock on *Olympic* that he, and Bruce Ismay, considered it inadvisable for the survivors to see the sister ship of *Titanic*, thus rejecting Haddock's offer to transfer the survivors to his own ship. At 7.47 p.m., *Carpathia* told *Olympic* that the captain, chief, first and sixth officers, and all engineers on *Titanic* had died, as well as the doctor, all pursers, one Marconi operator and the chief steward.

Rostron had earlier notified *Olympic* that *Titanic* had sunk and requested that, using her more powerful wireless, she relay the information to White Star, Cunard, Liverpool and New York. A tearful Phillip Franklin, Vice President of IMM, made the announcement to reporters in New York at 6.30 p.m.

Meanwhile, many of the *Carpathia* passengers had either given up or offered to share their accommodation with the survivors. Despite this, however, many of the rescued were forced to sleep in the various public rooms. To make matters worse, *Carpathia* was still required to separate the third-class survivors in order to satisfy the US immigration rules.

On the morning of Tuesday 16 April, several of the first-class survivors formed a committee to reward and thank Rostron and his crew, as well as to assist those who had lost family members or possessions.

J. Bruce Ismay, White Star Line's managing director, took refuge in the doctor's quarters and, after liaising with Rostron, sent a message to Franklin: 'Deeply regret advise you Titanic sank this morning after collision with iceberg, resulting in serious loss of life. Full particulars later. Bruce Ismay.' It is not known why this message, sent on the morning of 15 April, did not reach Franklin until the 17th, when he also received the following from Ismay: 'Very important you should hold Cedric daylight Friday for Titanic's crew. Answer. YAMSI.' Ismay's messaged attempt to get home to the UK as quickly as possible was intercepted by USS *Chester* and was sent on to Senator Smith, from Michigan, who had just been put in charge of the US Inquiry into the loss.

LIST OF

SALOON PASSENGERS

PER

S. S. "CARPATHIA,"

Commander - A. H. ROSTRON, R.D., R.N.R.

Surgeon - FRANK E. McGEE. Purser - E. G. F. BROWN, R.N.R·
Chief Steward E. H. HUGHES. Asst. Purser - P. B. BARNETT.

From Trieste to New York, Aug. 7th, 1912.
via Fiume, Patras, Naples, and Gibraltar.

Mrs S Anderson
Miss A W. Alvord
Mr A Ben Amslam
Miss K S Bassett
Miss C G Burt
Miss E H Burt
Miss Edith Burton
Miss Ethel Burton
Mr A P. Ball
Miss Bretz
Miss K L Blain
Mrs H M Blackburn
Mr T C Barr
Miss G M Bacon
Mr F B B Bostwick
Mrs Bostwick
Master W H Bostwick
Miss L Cockerill
Miss I I Closz
Miss T Corcoran
Mrs H G Cilley
Mr C B Carrier
Mrs C M Conden
Miss E M Clark
Miss G M Clark
Miss C S Cobb
Mrs W Cummings
Miss L T Colgan
Miss E G Colgan
Miss E L Call
Dr B A Camfield
Mrs Camfield
Mr R M Campbell
Mrs A M De Vall
Miss E Doleys
Mr A Doleys
Mrs M W Donnan
Miss M Donnan
Mrs J R Davis

Mr A C Dezendorf
Mr W Carr Dyer
Mrs Dyer
Miss C C Dyer
Dr C J Deeker
Mrs Decker
Miss M Decker

Miss E Ellison
Mr H P Elliott
Mr M C Early
Miss G East
Mrs J H Elward
Miss C Frei
Mr C E Foley
Mrs Foley
Mr L Foley
Mr R Foley
Mr C E Foley, Jr.
Master M Foley
Master A Foley
Miss B Floyd
Rev G H Ferris
Mrs Ferris
Mr N Frost
Miss J A Fowler
Mr Roger Foster
Mr W A Frayer
Dr H R Geyelin
Mr J B Gorham
Mrs Gorham
Mr N E Griffin
Miss J Glassock
Mrs G M Gibson
Rev W M Gordon
Miss M E Greig
Mr J Gatta
Miss J Gordon
Mr G H Goldsmith

Franklin replied that arrangements had already been made to return the crew on Saturday 20th on Red Star Line's *Lapland* and that it was considered to be 'most unwise' to delay the departure of *Cedric* under the circumstances.

In the *Marconi* room of *Carpathia* at 5 p.m., an exhausted Cottam was assisted by Harold Bride, who had to be carried into the cabin owing to the frostbite damage to his feet inflicted whilst aboard the upturned collapsible. Cottam later stated that, between the time of the rescue and the arrival in New York, he thought he had only had a maximum of ten hours sleep. The enormous number of free messages to be sent for the survivors only adding to the workload.

In New York, the press was eager for more information, as all that they had initially learnt was that *Titanic* had been in a collision with an iceberg and required assistance. Slowly, a list of first- and second-class survivors was sent to *Olympic* for onward dispatch. On Wednesday 17 April, Bride sent the names of third-class survivors on to USS *Chester*, dispatched by President Taft who was anxious for news of his aide Major Archibald Butt (lost), for relay to wireless stations ashore.

Rostron had commanded Cottam not to release any information about the disaster to the US press other than a list of survivors and, by the time *Carpathia* arrived in New York, the press was becoming increasingly frustrated by the lack of news.

U. S. S. CHESTER.

Above: The first page of a 1912 *Carpathia* passenger list showing Rostron in command.

Right: USS *Chester* was ordered by President Taft to meet *Carpathia*. (Muller)

LAPLAND

Built at Harland and Wolff, Belfast, the 18,694grt *Lapland* was ordered by the Antwerp-based Red Star Line and was completed in 1909. Carrying over 2,300 passengers, *Lapland* began operating her Antwerp–Dover–New York service in 1909. After the German invasion of Belgium at the beginning of the First World War, *Lapland* transferred to the UK and was operated by White Star Line, also a member of the International Mercantile Marine, mainly on the Liverpool–New York service. Several of White Star's vessels had been commandeered for war duties.

In January 1920, *Lapland* resumed her service from Antwerp to New York, operating a few Mediterranean cruises in 1932 and 1933. She was finally scrapped in Japan in 1934

Red Star Line's *Lapland* brought surviving crew back to the UK. (C.R. Hoffmann)

After experiencing thick fog during 17 April, *Carpathia* approached New York Harbor late on the evening of the 18th during a rainstorm. This did not deter the armada of small boats, filled with reporters, that greeted the Cunarder's arrival.

Surprising the waiting crowds and reporters, *Carpathia* proceeded to the White Star Line piers 59 and 60, where she paused to offload the thirteen *Titanic* lifeboats. The Merritt & Chapman tug *Champion* took them in tow and they were later placed in the loft of a building between piers 58 and 59, but their movements after this are not known. None of the Cunard passengers or rescued were permitted to disembark at Pier 59 and finally, at about 9.30 p.m., the vessel docked at Pier 54.

As *Carpathia* passed the battery at the southern end of Manhattan Island, a crowd of some 10,000 people had assembled near the Cunard pier at the end of West 14th Street. By the time the Cunarder had arrived at her company's own pier, that crowd had grown to over 30,000. Both forward and aft gangways were lowered and first to disembark were her own passengers, followed by the first-class survivors and those in second class shortly afterwards.

At about 11 p.m., the third-class survivors were allowed to disembark. The normal medical surveillance was restrained as a mark of respect and it is thought that they were amongst only a few New York-bound immigrants who were not processed through Ellis Island.

The surviving members of the crew, some 210 people, whose names had been transmitted to the US from *Carpathia* via Atlantic Transport Line's *Minnewaska*, finally disembarked around 11.30 p.m. To evade the news-hungry reporters, they were all shepherded to the US Immigration Service vessel *George Starr*, which took them to Pier 60, where they boarded Red Star Line's *Lapland* for the journey on Saturday 20 April to the UK. Many were eager to return to work as their pay had ceased when the waters of the North Atlantic closed over the stern of RMS *Titanic* on 15 April.

On Friday 19 April, Cunard Line's *Carpathia* departed New York at around 4 p.m. for the resumption of her journey to the Mediterranean.

twelve

POSTSCRIPT

QUESTIONS

As the ships of the White Star Line were popular with many Americans and due to such a high loss of life, it was only to be expected that the United States would hold an inquiry into the disaster.

Over 100 years has passed since the loss of the vessel and it will never be known exactly how many people were aboard her that night, nor exactly how many were saved. The generally accepted consensus of maritime historians is that 1,496 were lost and 712 saved, totalling some 2,208 souls. What is not in doubt, however, is the fact that the survival rates in first and second classes were much higher than in third class.

When *Titanic* left Queenstown on 11 April 1912 she was carrying 324 in first class of whom 201 were saved, and 118 of 284 second-class passengers made it to New York. Of the 709 third-class passengers carried, only 181 were saved, and those in third class who did not speak English represented a high proportion of the lost.

The crew numbered some 891 souls and only 212 were saved. Only 72 of the 325 in the engine department and 97 of the 500 in the victualling department were saved. Included in the crew total are the eight members of the ships' orchestra, five mail clerks, sixty-nine employed in the B deck (à la carte) restaurant, two wireless operators and the nine-man 'Guarantee Group' from Harland and Wolff. Of these, only two members of the restaurant staff and one wireless operator survived. Three of the ship's female crew of twenty-three were lost in the tragedy.

The total numbers lost were 1,340 of the 1,663 men, 109 of the 442 women and 47 of the 103 children, 46 of whom were in third class.

Despite the many flaws in each of the US and British inquiries, they still remain probably the best source of information for the serious researcher. The events of that dreadful night were still fresh in the mind of those witnesses giving evidence.

Olympic departed Southampton at 1.30 p.m. on 24 April, but many of her crew, questioning the removal of unnecessary lifeboats, refused to sail and, after protracted negotiations, the voyage was cancelled. *Olympic* returned on 26 April at 8.20 p.m. She is shown here laid up off Ryde, Isle of Wight, prior to her return to Southampton.

The US Inquiry began on 19 April 1912, the day after *Carpathia* arrived in New York. It was headed by William Alden Smith, the Republican senator from the state of Michigan, and finished on 25 May. Primarily held in the Senate in Washington DC, and occasionally in the Waldorf-Astoria hotel in New York, the US Inquiry was, in comparison to its British counterpart, informal and concentrated mostly on what had occurred. Senator Smith, ignorant of many nautical procedures, has been accused of straying off on a tangent on several occasions.

Despite J. Bruce Ismay's desire to return to the UK as quickly as possible, he was ordered to appear before the US Inquiry and only returned to Liverpool, departing on *Adriatic* in early May. The four surviving officers, hoping to return with Ismay, were also served with subpoenas demanding that they give evidence. Several members of the crew, including lookouts, were required to stay as witnesses, five of whom had already sailed on *Lapland* on Saturday 20 April. The vessel had to stop and the five were returned to New York by tug. One hundred and sixty-seven of the surviving crew then returned to the UK.

Many of those remaining as witnesses returned on *Celtic* from New York on Monday 29 April.

Captain Haddock, on *Olympic*, called on the captain of cruiser HMS *Cochrane* for assistance with the crew's refusal to sail. (Eisner)

"OLYMPIC" TRIPLE SCREW, 45,324 TONS.

THE LARGEST STEAMER IN THE WORLD

SOUTHAMPTON—CHERBOURG—QUEENSTOWN—NEW YORK SERVICE.
Via QUEENSTOWN (Westbound) via PLYMOUTH (Eastbound).

From Southampton.			From Cherbourg.	STEAMER	FROM NEW YORK. Calling at Plymouth and Cherbourg			From Southampton.			From Cherbourg.	STEAMER.	FROM NEW YORK. Calling at Plymouth and Cherbourg		
Date	Day.	Sailing Hour.	Date.		Date	Day	Sailing Hour.	Date.	Day.	Sailing Hour.	Date.		Date.	Day.	Sailing Hour.
1912 May 1	Wed.	Noon	May 1	*PHILADELPHIA	1912. May 11	Sat.	Noon	1912 Sept. 4	Wed.	Noon	Sept. 4	MAJESTIC	Sept. 14	Sat.	Noon
,, 8	Wed.	Noon	,, 8	OCEANIC	,, 18	Sat.	Noon.	,, 11	Wed.	Noon	,, 11	OCEANIC	,, 21	Sat.	Noon.
,, 15	Wed.	Noon	,, 15	OLYMPIC	,, 25	Sat.	1-0 pm	,, 18	Wed.	Noon	,, 18	OLYMPIC	,, 28	Sat.	Noon.
,, 22	Wed.	Noon	,, 22	MAJESTIC	June 1	Sat.	Noon.	,, 25	Wed.	Noon	,, 25	MAJESTIC	Oct. 5	Sat.	Noon
,, 29	Wed.	Noon	,, 29	OCEANIC	,, 8	Sat.	Noon.	Oct. 2	Wed.	Noon	Oct. 2	OCEANIC	,, 12	Sat.	Noon.
June 5	Wed.	Noon	June 5	OLYMPIC	,, 15	Sat.	10-0 am	,, 9	Wed.	Noon	,, 9	OLYMPIC	,, 19	Sat	Noon.
,, 12	Wed.	Noon	,, 12	MAJESTIC	,, 22	Sat.	Noon.	,, 16	Wed.	Noon	,, 16	MAJESTIC	,, 26	Sat.	Noon
,, 19	Wed.	Noon	,, 19	OCEANIC	,, 29	Sat.	Noon.	,, 23	Wed.	Noon	,, 23	OCEANIC	Nov. 2	Sat.	Noon.
,, 26	Wed.	11 am	,, 26	OLYMPIC	July 6	Sat.	Noon.	,, 30	Wed.	Noon	,, 30	OLYMPIC	,, 9	Sat.	10-0 am
July 3	Wed.	Noon	July 3	MAJESTIC	,, 13	Sat.	Noon	Nov. 6	Wed.	Noon	Nov. 6	MAJESTIC	,, 16	Sat.	Noon
,, 10	Wed.	Noon	,, 10	OCEANIC	,, 20	Sat.	Noon.	,, 13	Wed.	Noon	,, 13	OCEANIC	,, 23	Sat.	Noon.
,, 17	Wed.	Noon	,, 17	OLYMPIC	,, 27	Sat.	10-0 am	,, 20	Wed.	2-30 pm	,, 20	OLYMPIC	,, 30	Sat.	Noon.
,, 24	Wed.	Noon	,, 24	MAJESTIC	Aug. 3	Sat.	Noon	,, 27	Wed.	Noon	,, 27	MAJESTIC	Dec. 7	Sat.	Noon
,, 31	Wed.	Noon	,, 31	OCEANIC	,, 10	Sat.	Noon.	Dec. 4	Wed.	Noon	Dec. 4	OCEANIC	,, 14	Sat.	Noon
Aug. 7	Wed.	Noon	Aug. 7	OLYMPIC	,, 17	Sat.	Noon.	,, 11	Wed.	Noon	,, 11	OLYMPIC	,, 21	Sat.	3-0 pm
,, 14	Wed.	Noon	,, 14	MAJESTIC	,, 24	Sat.	Noon	,, 18	Wed.	Noon	,, 18	MAJESTIC	,, 28	Sat.	Noon
,, 21	Wed.	Noon	,, 21	OCEANIC	,, 31	Sat.	Noon.	,, 25	Wed.	Noon	,, 25	OCEANIC	1913 Jan. 4	Sat.	Noon
,, 28	Wed.	Noon	,, 28	OLYMPIC	Sept. 7	Sat.	2-0 pm								

SOUTHAMPTON PASSENGERS EMBARK AS FOLLOWS:—	First Class embark not later than	Second Class embark	Third Class embark	SPECIAL TRAINS. London to Southampton from Waterloo Station.		CHERBOURG. Passengers embark:—	
				For First Class	For Second and Third Cl.	All Classes	SPECIAL TRAIN PARIS to CHERBOURG from Gare St. Lazare.
For steamer sailing at 11 am	11 am	10 am	9-30 am	† 8-40 am	7-30 am	} about 4-30 pm	Train leaves Paris 9-40 am
,, ,, ,, Noon	Noon	11 am	10-30 am	† 9-45 am	8-30 am		
,, ,, ,, 2-30 pm	2 pm	1 pm	12-30 pm	† 10-40 am	9-30 am	} about 5-30 pm	Train leaves Paris 11 am

† Second Class Passengers can if more convenient leave Waterloo Station, London, by the Special train conveying First Class Passengers.

* American Line Steamer.

The evidence submitted by the witnesses could only represent a small amount of the events that occurred on board. Many of the witnesses were unreliable, and no third-class passengers were called to the US Inquiry.

The senior surviving officer, Lightoller, quite clearly defended his company, using expressions such as 'absence of swell' and 'circumstances you would not meet again in a hundred years'.

Left: White Star hastily issued a revised timetable, effective 1 May 1912.

Above: *Majestic* replaced the lost *Titanic* in the new timetable.

Lookout Frederick Fleet told the US Inquiry that, had he had binoculars, he would have seen the iceberg much earlier and that the disaster might have been averted. The bulk of opinion, however, is against him, believing that binoculars would have restricted his field of vision; however, lookouts were supposed to have been supplied with binoculars.

The British Inquiry began on 2 May 1912 and was headed by John Bigham (Lord Mersey), who would later go on to head the inquiries into the loss of *Empress of Ireland* in 1914 and *Lusitania* in 1915. This inquiry, much more formal than the American, was held at the Scottish Drill Hall in London and finished on 3 July. It was the British Board of Trade that held the inquiry and it was they who had allowed ships to sail with insufficient lifeboats for all on board!

The only passengers to testify at the British Inquiry were two of the twelve occupants of lifeboat 1, Sir Cosmo and Lady Duff Gordon. J. Bruce Ismay, one of those who decided that *Olympic* and *Titanic* would carry sixteen lifeboats under davits to satisfy the regulations rather than the suggested thirty-two or forty-eight, also appeared in the witness box.

At both inquiries it became clear that, on the North Atlantic, a practice had been followed for some two decades or more that speed was not reduced in the face of ice warnings and clear weather. Prior to the loss of *Titanic* no lives had been lost as a result of 'trusting to a good lookout' under these circumstances.

Captain Lord, and the crew of *Californian* that testified, emerged very unfavourably from both inquiries, with many contradictions and evasive answers to questions. Lord also gave misleading reports to the press whilst in the USA.

When the subject of barriers in third class arose, it became apparent that a few were locked but it was impossible to say which and where they were located.

When it became known that the White Star Line only paid its seagoing employees up to the time that the vessel sank, there was such a public outcry that the company did finally agree to pay the surviving crew for the time that they were away from the UK.

On the whole, the findings of both inquiries were similar in that *Titanic* was steaming at nearly her top speed into a known ice area and the only precaution taken was to say to the lookouts 'keep a sharp lookout for ice'.

Unavoidably, the lack of sufficient lifeboat accommodation was mentioned, as well as criticism of the loading procedure. This was dealt with by the US Inquiry in much greater detail, Senator Smith describing the 'laxity of regulation and hasty inspection' by the British Board of Trade as the major contributor to the loss of life. The Board of Trade concluded, unsurprisingly, that they were not to blame, stating that the disaster was 'brought about by the excessive speed at which the ship was being navigated'.

The US Senate Inquiry submitted its final report into the disaster on 28 May 1912. In it they made the following recommendations: there were to be sufficient lifeboats to accommodate all on board; at least four crew members should be allocated to each boat; drills were to be carried out at least twice a month; and both passengers and crew should be assigned to a lifeboat. A wireless operator should be on duty at all times, thus requiring two operators on each ship, and they should have direct communication with the bridge. Rockets should only be fired at sea to indicate distress. Bulkheads should be raised to ensure that they reach the uppermost continual structured deck, thus ensuring that the compartment formed became watertight.

The recommendations resulting from the British Inquiry were basically the same except, additionally: company regulations should require that vessels slow down in known ice regions and captains should be aware that it is an offence not to go to the aid of a vessel in distress.

Many believe that this final requirement was aimed directly at Captain Lord of *Californian* and that the British Board of Trade used him as a scapegoat, thus evading the issue that it was they who had permitted *Titanic*, and indeed all British ships over 10,000 tons, to sail with insufficient life-saving capabilities.

It is often, erroneously, thought that the lifeboats in the foreground come from *Titanic*. Her boats did, in fact, disappear in New York and their whereabouts remains a mystery. *Olympic* is in the background. (Ashfield)

The ageing *Majestic*, seen here at Southampton taken out of reserve to fill the gap in the schedule.

The recommendations of both inquiries unquestionably required major changes to British maritime regulations, but such changes only took place over a substantial period of time and were, to say the least, piecemeal.

The discovery of the wreck in September 1985 supported those fourteen who testified that they saw the ship break before sinking. Four witnesses at the inquiries, including two of the officers, said that the vessel remained intact as she went down. Despite several stating that the vessel broke apart prior to sinking, both inquiries also found that the vessel went down whole.

On 12 November 1913, the International Convention on the Safety of Life at Sea (SOLAS) met for the first time in London. Composed predominantly of those countries that had ships operating on the North Atlantic, power was limited until more nations and shipping companies joined the organisation. Two of the articles from this first convention came as a direct result of the loss of *Titanic*. The use of any signals at night that might be confused with distress signals was banned and all engine-driven vessels over 50m long were to display two steaming lights. This last condition would prevent any large liner from being mistaken for a smaller tramp steamer.

IN MEMORIAM

On Friday 19 April 1912, the first of several memorial services was held at St Paul's Cathedral in London. Amongst the more than 5,000 attendees was Alexander Carlisle, the man initially responsible for the design of the Olympic-class liners at Harland and Wolff in Belfast. Almost twice as many were outside.

The vessels chartered by the White Star Line to recover as many bodies as possible from the disaster site returned to Halifax, Nova Scotia, bearing their grim cargo. Many of the bodies were so badly damaged that they were buried at sea. Over fifty of the dead were returned to family and friends for private burial and the remaining 150, forty-four of whom were identifiable, were interred in three cemeteries in Halifax.

The majority – 121 – of the recovered victims of the disaster were buried in the Fairview Lawn Cemetery, whereas nineteen Catholics were interred in the Mount Olivet Cemetery. The Baron de Hirsch Jewish Cemetery holds ten graves. The White Star Line established a trust, which is still responsible for the maintenance of the graves.

London's St Paul's Cathedral held a memorial service less than a week after the disaster.

ST. PAUL'S CATHEDRAL.

FRIDAY, 19TH APRIL, 1912,
AT 12 NOON.

Memorial Service

FOR

THOSE WHO PERISHED THROUGH THE
FOUNDERING OF THE SS. "TITANIC"

ON

MONDAY, APRIL 15TH, 1912.

REQUIEM MASS AT WESTMINSTER CATHEDRAL.

All Saints' Parish Church,
SOUTHAMPTON.

✝

SUNDAY, April 21st,

1912.

✠ ✠

The Loss of the White Star
Liner "Titanic."

WARREN & SON, STEAM PRINTERS, SOUTHAMPTON.

Sacred to the Memory of
1,635 Heroes

who lost their lives in mid-Atlantic, through
the great liner,

"TITANIC,"

colliding with an Iceberg, on the Sabbath
night of April 14, 1912.

Thro' the darkness of the night came a call,
The call of death that told them all was o'er.
Before their God in silence they did fall,
And landed safely on a brighter shore.

LORD, if it be Thy command that we should
leave so suddenly those we love, may it please
Thee to bring us together in heaven.

NEARER MY GOD TO THEE.

HARRY SIMMONS, Truro, May, 1912.

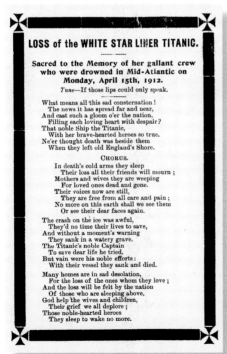

LOSS of the WHITE STAR LINER TITANIC.

Sacred to the Memory of her gallant crew
who were drowned in Mid-Atlantic on
Monday, April 15th, 1912.

Tune—If those lips could only speak.

What means all this sad consternation!
    The news it has spread far and near,
And cast such a gloom o'er the nation,
    Filling each loving heart with despair?
That noble Ship the Titanic,
    With her brave-hearted heroes so true.
Ne'er thought death was beside them
    When they left old England's Shore.

CHORUS.

In death's cold arms they sleep
    Their loss all their friends will mourn ;
Mothers and wives they are weeping
    For loved ones dead and gone.
Their voices now are still,
    They are free from all care and pain ;
No more on this earth shall we see them
    Or see their dear faces again.

The crash on the ice was awful,
    They'd no time their lives to save,
And without a moment's warning
    They sank in a watery grave.
The Titanic's noble Captain
    To save dear life he tried,
But vain were his noble efforts :
    With their vessel they sank and died.

Many homes are in sad desolation,
    For the loss of the ones whom they love ;
And the loss will be felt by the nation
    Of those who are sleeping above.
God help the wives and children,
    Their grief we all deplore ;
Those noble-hearted heroes
    They sleep to wake no more.

Das entsetzliche Dampfer-Unglück.

Der Untergang des Dampfers „Titanic"
des schönsten und größten Dampfers der Welt
am 15. April 1912, Nachts 2 Uhr 26.

Top left: A Requiem Mass was held at London's Westminster Cathedral. (J. Beagles / private collection)

Top centre: Southampton's All Saints parish church held a memorial service on the Sunday following the disaster.

Top right: Many black-bordered memorial cards were issued immediately after the disaster. The number lost was later revised downwards.

Far left: Hymns and poems proliferated on postcards.

Left: A postcard issued at the time in Germany, detailing the disaster.

129

One of several memorial cards issued at the time. The illustration shows *Titanic* departing Belfast on her trials.

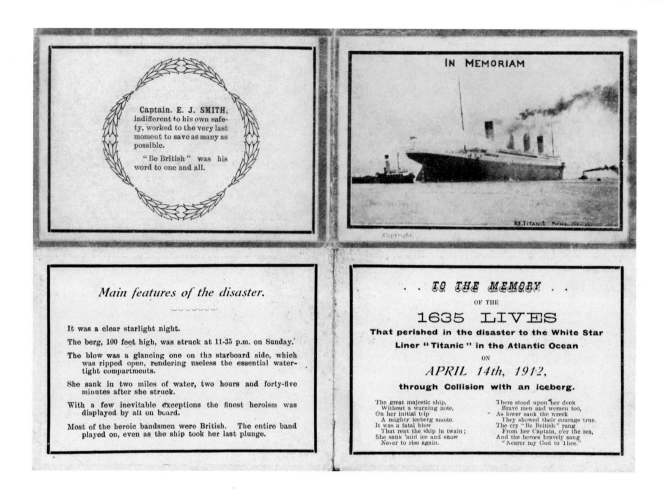

Captain. E. J. SMITH, indifferent to his own safety, worked to the very last moment to save as many as possible.

"Be British" was his word to one and all.

IN MEMORIAM

Main features of the disaster.

It was a clear starlight night.

The berg, 100 feet high, was struck at 11-35 p.m. on Sunday.

The blow was a glancing one on the starboard side, which was ripped open, rendering useless the essential watertight compartments.

She sank in two miles of water, two hours and forty-five minutes after she struck.

With a few inevitable exceptions the finest heroism was displayed by all on board.

Most of the heroic bandsmen were British. The entire band played on, even as the ship took her last plunge.

.. TO THE MEMORY ..
OF THE
1635 LIVES
That perished in the disaster to the White Star Liner "Titanic" in the Atlantic Ocean
ON
APRIL 14th, 1912,
through Collision with an iceberg.

The great majestic ship,
Without a warning note,
On her initial trip
A mighty iceberg smote.
It was a fatal blow
That rent the ship in twain;
She sank 'mid ice and snow
Never to rise again.

There stood upon her deck
Brave men and women too,
As lower sank the wreck
They showed their courage true.
The cry "Be British" rang
From her Captain, o'er the sea,
And the heroes bravely sang
"Nearer my God to Thee."

A memorial performance was held at London's Royal Opera House on Tuesday 14 May 1912, attended by King George V and Queen Mary. Among the many artists appearing at the concert were actress Sarah Bernhardt and dancer Anna Pavlova.

On 24 May, the Titanic Band Memorial Concert was held at the Royal Albert Hall in London. Sir Henry Wood conducted an orchestra of almost 500, and amongst the repertoire was the hymn *Nearer my God to Thee*.

One year after the disaster, on 15 April 1913, a service of dedication was held at the Seamen's Church Institute of New York. The subject of the dedication was a memorial lighthouse located on the roof of the institute. On the top of the lighthouse was a black ball that dropped every day at 1 p.m., and a green light, visible from New York Harbor, was installed. In 1968 the building was demolished and the Titanic Memorial Lighthouse was transferred to its permanent location at the South Street Seaport Museum.

On 29 April 1914, in Southampton, a large crowd of people witnessed the dedication of probably the best known of that city's memorials. The Engineer Officers' Memorial, located in East Park, carries a bronze statue

TITANIC MEMORIAL, SOUTHAMPTON.

The railings in front of the famous Engineers' Memorial in Southampton were removed during the First World War and never replaced. (Philco / private collection)

In Sacred Memory of

The "TITANIC"

WHICH COLLIDED WITH AN ICEBERG

OFF CAPE RACE, on APRIL 15th, 1912.

The most appalling disaster in Maritime History

with a loss of over 1,500 lives.

She struck where the white and fleecy waves,
  Looked soft as carded wool,
But the cruel rocks, they gored her side,
  Like the horns of an angry bull.

Her rattling shrouds, all sheathed in ice,
  With the masts went by the board,
Like a vessel of glass, she stove and sank,
  Ho! Ho! the breakers roared.

Printed & Published by The East London Printing Co.,
7, Houndsditch, London, E.C.

Thy Will be done

This memorial card illustrates *Titanic* departing Southampton. (East London Printing Co.)

131

Right: New York's lighthouse memorial, now situated at the South Street Seaport Museum. (Artvue / private collection)

Far right: The Southampton memorial to the fireman and crew of *Titanic*. (Rood Bros)

Titanic Memorial Tower, Seamen's Church
Institute of New York, 25 South Street

Titanic Firemen & Crew Memorial,
Southampton Common

of Nike, the winged goddess of victory, and commemorates the thirty-five engineers who lost their lives in the disaster. Nearby, on a wall plaque, is a memorial to the eight musicians of the ship's orchestra and in the Civic Centre in Southampton there is a memorial to the five postal workers, all of whom also lost their lives.

The crew memorial fountain was dedicated, in a Southampton park, on 27 July 1915, but on 15 April 1972, sixty years after the disaster, the fountain, threatened by weather and vandalism, was moved to a new permanent location in the ruined Holy Rood church. This church had been the victim of German bombers in the Second World War and the ruins also serve as a commemoration to those seamen of Britain's merchant marine who lost their lives in wartime.

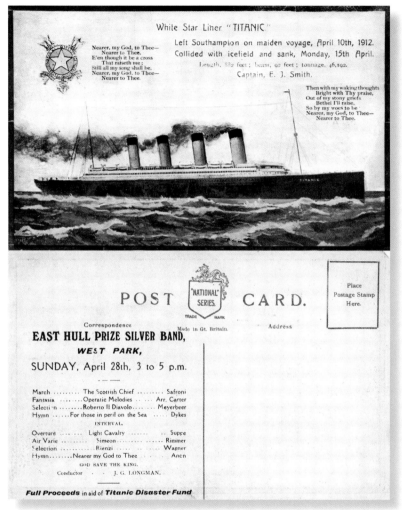

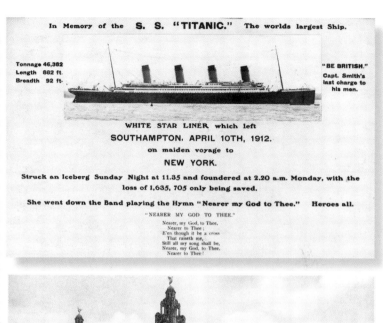

Titanic Memorial and Liver Buildings, Liverpool

In St Joseph's church on Bugle Street, Southampton, is a memorial dedicated to Luigi Gatti and the waiters of the B deck (à la carte) restaurant.

A bronze memorial statue of Captain Edward Smith is located in Beacon Park, Lichfield, in Staffordshire. Created by the sculptress Lady Kathleen Scott, widow of 'Scott of the Antarctic', the statue was unveiled by Smith's daughter, Helen, on 29 July 1914. There is no mention of *Titanic* on the memorial but it carries the words 'Be British'.

Another memorial to the engineers was erected in the White Star Line's homeport of Liverpool, near the Prince's Landing Stage and the Royal Liver Building on the river Mersey. Later, the design also incorporated those engineers killed during the First World War.

Above left: A concert, given by the East Hull Prize Silver Band in aid of the disaster fund, is advertised on the reverse of a memorial postcard.

Top right: *Titanic* is shown departing Southampton on this memorial postcard. (Debenham)

Above: Liverpool's memorial outside the Liver Buildings.

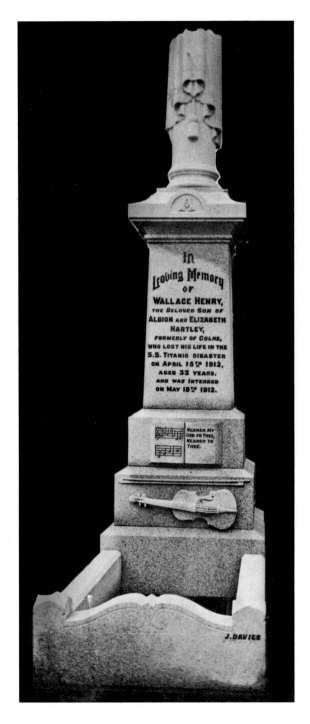

GODALMING CHURCH AND PHILLIPS MEMORIAL.

The bodies of three members of the ship's orchestra were recovered from the North Atlantic and that of bandleader and violinist Wallace Hartley was interred in a cemetery in Colne, Lancashire. A memorial has been erected there in his memory.

Next to the church of St Peter and St Paul in Godalming, Surrey, is a large cloister and gardens dedicated to the senior Marconi operator, Jack Phillips.

Nineteen years after the tragedy, in 1931, Mrs Taft unveiled the Women's Titanic Memorial in Rock Creek Park, Washington DC. Many women had donated $1 each in contribution to the construction of the memorial honouring those men who had given their lives in sacrifice for the women and children of *Titanic*. The memorial was moved in 1968 to the present location on 'P' street SW.

Left: The grave of Wallace Hartley at Colne.

Above: The memorial to senior Marconi operator Jack Phillips at Godalming. His body was not recovered. (A. Jury / private collection)

Archie Butt Memorial Bridge, Augusta, Ga.

The Memorial Bridge, in Augusta, Georgia, dedicated to President Taft's aide Major Archibald Butt, who was lost in the disaster. His body was not recovered. (Albion News)

AFTER THE DISASTER

The loss of *Titanic* obviously left a gap in the White Star Line's sailing schedule. Had she arrived in New York on Tuesday 16 April, her return departure would have commenced at 12 noon on Saturday 20 April. The next westbound departure, from Southampton, had been allocated to *Olympic* on Wednesday 24 April.

A hastily revised timetable was issued effective from 1 May 1912 and the American Line's *Philadelphia* is shown as operating the Wednesday 1 May sailing from Southampton to New York. She was sister to the liner *New York*, which had snapped her mooring ropes as *Titanic* departed Southampton on 10 April. It was *Oceanic* that left Southampton with the 8 May sailing. *Olympic* was shown, in the revised schedule, as taking the 15 May Southampton departure.

As the busy summer of 1912 drew to a close, *Olympic* returned to Belfast for extensive alterations in addition to her annual overhaul. Prior to this, and after the loss of her sister, her passenger loads had fallen considerably; despite the green shoots of recovery beginning to appear in public confidence, it was quite apparent that changes were required.

Above: The keel of *Britannic*, the third ship of the class, had been laid down on 30 November 1911 on Slip No. 2, which had been vacated by *Olympic*.

Above: White Star advertised the 'New Olympic' in 1913 after her extensive refit in Belfast.

Probably the most important was the raising of five watertight bulkheads to just below B deck, thus ensuring that the vessel would stay afloat with up to six continuous compartments open to the sea. An inner skin, under the engine and boiler areas, was fitted which predominantly embraced the length of the vessel.

These changes had already been made on the third Olympic-class vessel, *Britannic*, still being built at Belfast. Both vessels were also provided with an indicator advising the bridge that all the watertight doors had been closed. No such indicator had been aboard *Titanic*.

It is often thought that the loss of *Titanic* resulted in a policy of 'lifeboats for all'. This was not necessarily so, as, in many cases on vessels at the time, the existing davits were not designed to launch more than one lifeboat. Even today a vessel may put to sea providing that she is fitted with lifeboats for up to 75 per cent of her passenger and crew capacity. She must also carry life rafts, satisfying specified conditions and with launching facilities, for 25 per cent, as well as further life rafts for another 25 per cent, but it is not necessary for these last rafts to have their own launch capability.

The London & South Western Railway station at Southampton Docks gave access to the South Western Hotel, where J. Bruce Ismay, his family and Thomas Andrews stayed overnight on 9 April. The hotel now comprises apartments and the station has been converted into a casino.

The buildings on the dockside adjacent to the Southampton berth were badly damaged during a Second World War bombing raid and, after demolition, were replaced by the Ocean Terminal that was torn down in 1983.

BRITANNIC (II)

Bruce Ismay, Chairman and Managing Director of the White Star Line, on board the maiden voyage of his company's new liner, RMS *Olympic*, was so impressed with his ship that he decided to confirm the option for a third vessel of the class. The new vessel, to be named *Britannic*, was ordered on 20 June 1911 and she was launched on a wet and cold 26 February 1914. Construction work was suspended pending the results of the American and British inquiries into the loss of *Titanic*.

Work recommenced with the recommended increased watertight subdivisions, double skin and improved lifeboat capacity for all on board. Her planned capacity was to be 790 first-, 836 second- and 953 third-class passengers with a crew of 950.

After the declaration of war on 4 August 1914, *Britannic* was requisitioned for hospital duties on 13 November 1915. Her white-painted hull was surrounded by a large green band broken by three red crosses on each side and her four funnels, slightly shorter than those of her sisters, were painted a buff colour without the familiar black top of the White Star Line.

Having made five return wartime voyages to the Mediterranean, she left Southampton, mercifully empty of wounded, on 12 November 1916 for Mudros. En route, *Britannic* ran on to a minefield, in the Zea Channel, laid by German submarine *U73*, at 8.12 a.m. on 21 November. Captain Bartlett, in a vain attempt to beach his wounded vessel, restarted the engines. The still-turning propellers, as they began to emerge from the water, destroyed two lifeboats.

Britannic sank at 9.07 a.m. with the loss of thirty-four lives. The wreck lies on its starboard side in the Zea Channel and, to this day, remains the largest ever wartime loss of a ship in the British merchant service.

Unsere Lebensmittelschiffe im Hamburger Hafen.

Der 64 000 To.-Riesendampfer „Bismarck", das größte Schiff der Welt, daneben ein 20 000 To.- Dampfer.

Bismarck, the last of three giant German liners larger than the Olympic class, lay incomplete in Hamburg during the First World War and was ceded to Britain, as White Star's *Majestic 2*, in 1922.

Cunard's answer to the Olympic-class vessels: RMS *Aquitania* (1914–50). (E.A. Sweetman)

White Star's first *Majestic* being scrapped at Morecambe in 1914. (Sankey)

Napoleon was initially responsible for the creation of Cherbourg as an important harbour facility but, in 1912, it was still not large enough to handle a ship the size of *Titanic*, so it had been necessary to send passengers out to waiting vessels in tenders. Cherbourg continued to grow and became one of France's most important departure points for migrants from all over the Old World.

Queenstown, in Southern Ireland, became Cobh after Irish independence in 1922 and, at the same time, Kingstown, on the east coast near Dublin, was renamed Dun Loaghaire.

Lookout Frederick Fleet, who had been the first to see the iceberg, retired from the sea in 1955. He became a newspaper seller in Southampton and, on 10 January 1965, after the death of his wife, he committed suicide.

Second Officer Lightoller, who had steadfastly defended the White Star Line at both the US and British Inquiries, is believed to have thought that the US Senate Subcommittee hearing was nothing but a farce. He died in December 1952.

Fourth officer on board *Titanic*, Joseph Boxhall went on to serve the merged Cunard-White Star Line as senior first officer and is seen here on their *Aquitania* in an advertisement for the company. (Cunard Line)

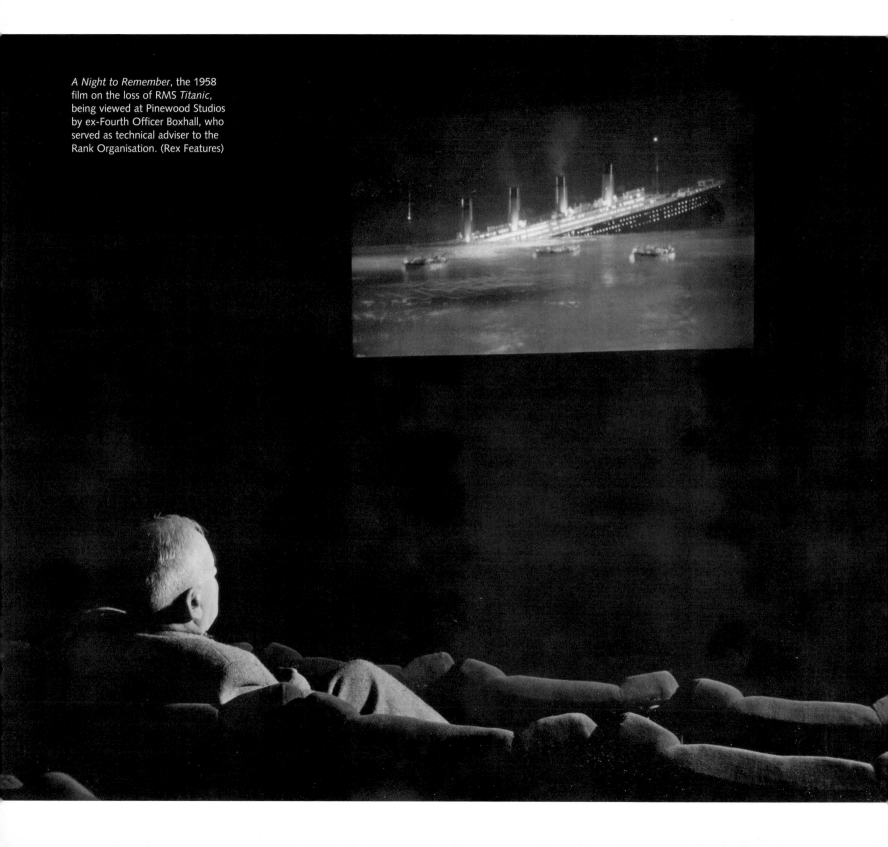

A Night to Remember, the 1958 film on the loss of RMS *Titanic*, being viewed at Pinewood Studios by ex-Fourth Officer Boxhall, who served as technical adviser to the Rank Organisation. (Rex Features)

Third Officer Herbert Pitman, with deteriorating eyesight, is thought to have transferred to the purser's office around 1920.

Fifth Officer Lowe, despite his attempts to rescue people from the water, was not suitably rewarded or recognised by the White Star Line. He served as third officer on board their lesser passenger-cargo vessel *Medic* and died in 1944 at the age of 61.

Fourth Officer Boxhall retired from the sea in 1940 at the age of 56. He had served as an officer on board Cunard-White Star Line's *Aquitania* in the mid 1930s and, in 1957, provided technical assistance to the Rank Organisation in the making of their film *A Night to Remember*, based on Walter Lord's book of the same name, about the loss of *Titanic*. He died in 1967, at the age of 83, and at his request his ashes were scattered over the position of *Titanic*, 41.46 N, 50.14 W, which he had calculated back in 1912.

The majority of vessels referred to were eventually broken up except:

Britannic, *Californian*, *Carpathia*, *Cincinnati*, *La Provence*, *Laurentic*, *Lusitania*, *Mesaba*, *Minnewaska* and *Mount Temple* which were lost during the First World War.
Asian, *Celtic*, *Oceanic* and *Ypiranga* wrecked, becoming total losses.
Medic and *Traffic* lost during the Second World War.
Nomadic is preserved today in Belfast.

France, the only four-funnelled French liner, made her maiden transatlantic voyage a week after the loss of *Titanic*. She was broken up in 1936.

White Star's *Celtic* ran aground off Roches Point near Cobh (Queenstown) in 1928 and was broken up in situ in 1933.

The ageing *Mauretania*, painted white in a vain attempt at cruising, was eventually broken up in 1935.

SINKING OF THE "KAISER WILHELM DER GROSSE" BY H.M.S. HIGHFLYER

One of Germany's early transatlantic greyhounds, *Kaiser Wilhelm der Grosse*, sunk early in the First World War. (Regent Publishing)

KRONPRINZESSIN CECILIE AT BAR HARBOR ME.

Kronprinzessin Cecilie, disguised as *Olympic*, was interned by the USA at the start of the First World War and, in 1917, became the troopship USS *Mount Vernon*.

R.M.S. "*Lusitania.*"

Lusitania, which was torpedoed and sunk in 1915 with fearful loss of life. (Valentine's)

Britannic never served as a passenger liner and was lost to a mine in the Aegean while in service as a hospital ship in 1916. (Nautical)

Mount Temple, shown here aground off Nova Scotia, was sunk by a German surface raider during the First World War.

Mesaba was torpedoed and sunk during the First World War.

S. S. "Mesaba"   Atlantic Transport Co.

BIBLIOGRAPHY

de Kerbrech, Richard, *Ships of the White Star Line* (Ian Allan, 2009)

Eaton, John P., and Charles A. Haas, *Titanic: Triumph and Tragedy* (Patrick Stephens Ltd, 1986)

Fitch, Tad, J. Kent Layton and Bill Wormstedt, *On a Sea of Glass: The Life and Loss of the RMS Titanic* (Amberley Publishing, 2012)

Halpern, Sam, et al., *Report into the Loss of the SS Titanic: A Centennial Reappraisal* (The History Press, 2012)

Haws, Duncan, *Merchant Fleets in Profile 2: The Ships of the Cunard, American, Red Star, Inman, Leyland, Dominion, Atlantic Transport and White Star Lines* (Patrick Stephens Ltd, 1979)